FEWER RULES, BETTER PEOPLE

NORTON
SHORTS

FEWER RULES, BETTER PEOPLE

The Case for Discretion

BARRY LAM

W. W. NORTON & COMPANY
Independent Publishers Since 1923

For information about special discounts for bulk purchases, please
contact W. W. Norton Special Sales at specialsales@wwnorton.com or
800-233-4830

Manufacturing by Lakeside Book Company
Production manager: Delaney Adams

ISBN 978-1-324-05124-4

W. W. Norton & Company, Inc.
500 Fifth Avenue, New York, NY 10110
www.wwnorton.com

W. W. Norton & Company Ltd.
15 Carlisle Street, London W1D 3BS

10 9 8 7 6 5 4 3 2 1

To Darcy: May you grow up wise and discerning, when all the forces seem to militate against it.

CONTENTS

FEWER RULES, BETTER PEOPLE

INTRODUCTION

BESIDES DEATH AND TAXES, the third great certainty about civilized life is *bureaucracy*. You cannot live or die without submitting proper paperwork to the proper authorities. Be born without a birth certificate and you will not exist. Die without a death certificate and you will continue to owe money to a government unable to recognize that you no longer exist. Try to earn, win, or even give away any significant amount of money and you will need to fill out some series of forms, pay some kind of administrative fee, and stand in some line. And when you need something important in life, a range of numbers with coded meaning will zip between bureaucrats, informing them of some positive or negative aspect of your identity, like your credit or LSAT scores, your criminal risk assessment grade, your occupational licensing status, your immunization record, and on and on. Someone behind the scenes is always looking at whether your papers are in order, and they will be returned for resubmission if they do not have an ink-dried, notarized signature on page three. And that would be if you're lucky. More often than not, if you commit an oversight, your papers are simply discarded for being improper, and you only find that out when you show up for an important appointment and find you are not in the system. And so you are asked to start again.

Governments and the private sector, low-stakes institutions and high-stakes ones are all beholden to rules, policies, procedures, regulations, and the bureaucrats who implement them. It isn't just the government, it is your wireless carrier, your utility company, your bank, and your school—any organization of scale walks down the path of bureaucratization and then over-bureaucratization. Big businesses, small businesses that compete with big businesses, community groups, youth sports, and anything involving the management of lots of people will require rules and their enforcement, rather than informal exchanges between people built on trust, friendships, acquaintanceships, and verbal agreements.

As I sit down to write this chapter, my wife calls, needing me to go through our file drawer. A nurse at one of the country's largest healthcare providers is unable to administer the second of a two-shot vaccine series to my ten-year-old daughter during an appointment specifically scheduled by the provider for the second shot. There is no record in their system of the first shot. I understand things from the health care provider's perspective. You can't trust a patient's word about their vaccine history. How often are they wrong? And how many patients want to lie about their vaccine history to avoid getting boosters? And god forbid, what if you have a nurse or doctor who takes bribes to help patients falsify their medical records, not only to get out of routine vaccines, but to get worker's compensation, cheaper life insurance policies, or to pass drug tests for jobs? There's a reason why the medical system introduces procedural and computerized safeguards against mistakes and fraud, especially ones that can lead to liabilities.

It doesn't matter that crooked doctors, anti-vaccine parents, and health record fraudsters are incredibly rare. One scandal is enough to cause major procedural reactions. It is built into the evolutionary structure of organizations of scale to encounter problems and liabilities and to fix them by formulating a new rule sent out by memo for other people to implement. It is part of that same evolution for someone somewhere to find a loophole in the rule, leading to an additional clause, culminating in dozens of pages of fine print, and then a computer system that collects, organizes, and sends information in accordance with those rules. Rules and procedures are the order of the day when any organization gets large enough. And in litigious societies, like the US, these rules better be in writing and reviewed by the modern-day clergy of rule making, lawyers.

Rage at the burdens of regulation drives conservative and libertarian anger. The proliferation of all these forms, rules, regulations, and computer systems, and the bureaucrats who design and enforce them, are generally associated with the liberal state. And it is true that in the government, many such rules are implemented in the service of a safer, fairer, and more predictable society, the hallmark of classical liberalism. But liberals rage at bureaucracy too, and plenty of conservatives and conservative institutions, like businesses big and small, play their part in designing their own set of burdensome rules and procedures.

No matter who you are, there are good chances that you are at least sometimes a bureaucrat. It may even be your full-time job. I am one. I enter student grades on a spreadsheet, formulate or relay university rules to them about laptops, cheating, and enrollment procedures, and I click on drop-down menus to issue reports about myself and others. Whether you are in car sales, library administration, shipping logistics, teaching, learning, even parking, if you deal with records, quality control, credit scores, receipts, databases, standardized tests, or GPAs, you are a bureaucrat. We are all as much agents of the bureaucracy as we are subjects to it.

Societies like ours were anticipated, and even advocated, by political philosophers as far back as 300 BCE in ancient China, a school of thought called Legalism (with a capital L). According to Legalism, the ideal of civil society is where everyone—citizens, enforcers, and bureaucrats who oversee segments of society—operates under a system of policy, procedure, and law, written down for all to read and follow, with compliance officers holding everyone to account. Legalism was meant to unify hundreds of warring ethnic groups into a single society. It required a ruthless dictatorial regime to ensure total compliance. The smooth functioning and predictability of civil life was the ideal.

Today, legalism (with a lower-case l) is triumphant: the idea that organizations are best governed by detailed rules structured in a bureaucracy of managers, enforcers, and compliance officers, where even high-level rulers are subject to some form of law and procedure. Regardless of where a society lies on the political or economic spectrum—democratic or totalitarian, capitalistic or socialistic—we are all bound by the perceived need for rules and standard procedures. This form of legalism is a descendant of both ancient Chinese Legalism and Western liberalism. For liberals, legalism is less about the quality of governance and more about its moral character. Liberals believe we need to be rule governed lest we devolve into a culture of corruption, nepotism, favors, and arbitrary exercises of power by individuals, all features we associate with unjust societies and failed states.

Bureaucracy in theory is supposed to be an essential solution to problems of social organization, but in practice it often leads to a frustrated citizen staring incredulously at a helpless worker in a system with no good choices among a mountain of rules. Knowledge of 2,500 years of political philosophical history brings me no closer to solving the problem with the nurse and the vaccine. But a trick built into bureaucratic organizations can solve problems like mine immediately. No matter how complicated a rule, procedure, policy, or computerized system, you can build into the job of implementing rules a way for people to break or ignore them without risking sanction. You give bureaucrats *discretion*. And you make sure wise bureaucrats exercise it.

Luckily for me and my child, the nurse found a way to administer the shot, record it, and prevent herself from getting into trouble. The nurse had discretion to issue something called "historical entry," allowing her to start some paperwork to be submitted for subsequent review. We are not always so lucky when we interact with a bureaucracy. I have a notepad filled with stories of people failing to navigate bureaucracies in their own workplaces, with the government, with utility companies, pretty much everywhere. The result is frustration or catastrophe, depending on how much discretion bureaucrats are allowed to have.

Where there is bureaucracy, there is some discretion. How much discretion and how it is used are behind just about everything good, bad, and ugly in civil society.

Is discretion good or bad? In designing a workplace, a household, a criminal justice system, or a society, should we seek to minimize or maximize the discretionary authority of the bureaucrats who will ultimately run those institutions? This is the central question I ask in this book, and there are two ways of trying to answer it. The scientific approach compares two organizations, one where bureaucrats have a lot of discretion and one where they do not, to find which organization does better. Maybe the police department in small town A gives officers a choice of whether to make arrests for petty theft, while small town B makes arrest mandatory, leaving officers zero discretion. Which town has less petty theft?

The answer turns out to be complicated. The area in which discretion has been studied a lot is US criminal justice, where natural and imposed experiments abound. The US criminal justice system has oscillated between periods of high discretion and high top-down management. It has also oscillated between high-crime and low-crime periods, as well as times of good and bad criminal justice outcomes. How are we to know whether the good times are the result of discretionary decision making or something else, like a good or bad economy or whether there is clean rather than tainted tap water? Secondly, there are many things we mean by *good* and *bad*. A city that gives more discretion to its traffic officers might mean more warnings and fewer tickets for speeding, and this increases good will toward the police in the community, which is good. But it also might lead to non-white drivers being issued more tickets than white drivers, which is bad.

So overall, from a scientific perspective, is discretion better? Case studies give a mixed answer. Strictly scientific ways of trying to answer a normative question about a very complex matter tend to fall short. Normative questions are about human values, and what humans value about governments, institutions, and organizations are as complex as those institutions. There are alternative philosophical ways to seek an answer, appealing to first principles rather than looking at the large and messy world of policy.

The legalist tradition unambiguously argues that discretion is bad—that it gives too much power to those in charge, making for a society of laws, except for the ones the people in power choose to ignore. When the people in power are benevolent and wise, there might be some good outcomes, but overall, giving discretion to individuals to circumvent the predictability and fairness of rules is not a good idea. According to legalism, to the extent that discretion must exist, it is because we formulate imperfect rules, something we do because we are imperfect rule makers. At best, discretion is a necessary evil. But it is always an evil, to be done away with as societies evolve to be morally, technologically, and economically more advanced.

Even libertarians, who are no fans of burdensome and complex rules, believe that discretion is bad. Top-down authority in general is suspicious, so more top-down authority given to bureaucrats is an evil. The less power we impose on the citizenry, the better. However, libertarians have no problem with rules, procedures, and constraints imposed on government officials. In the view of libertarians, whether some government bureaucrat is allowed to intervene in a criminal justice matter or in a free-market matter requires rules that are quite elaborate, even legalistic. Similarly, in the anarchist left, where direct democracy is an ideal, no one should have special authority to sidestep or bend rules. No one should have discretion. That would be to give a member of the community unequal power, a most repugnant state of affairs in an anarchic society. But even in anarchy, there must be rules on organized decision-making. How many people must be present for a quorum, how long is debate allowed, how much time is each person given, what are the procedures for closing debate and calling for a vote, what is the voting procedure, and what is the procedure for changing the voting procedure? Even the anarchist must sometimes be a legalist.

Much political philosophy has converged on the idea that we must move away from the whims and wills of enforcers in order to have functional and morally legitimate institutions. The best places to live and work, the best hospitals, and the best schools for our children are the ones with the best policies and rules. And according to legalists, the best rules do not make room for discretionary decisions to ignore or bend those rules.

Legalism is a pervasive feature of modern life, a default tendency in our thinking that explains why there is so much criminal law and fine print and so many handbooks of procedure, clauses in the school dress code, and receipts to keep on file. The thinking behind legalism and the tendency for organizations to evolve toward legalistic thinking is powerful.

Yet I would like to make a case against legalism, in favor of more discretion. We need fewer rules and better people. In my view, discretion is not a necessary evil to be minimized and ultimately discarded when technology and economics allow us to blindly implement a fully rule-based society. Instead, I think discretion is a constitutive feature of a well-run institution that seeks to maximize fairness, justice, efficiency, and effectiveness. It is good that there is a nurse making a judgment call about whether to violate a rule. It is good for her patient, good for her, good for her organization, and good for society at large that she has this power.

If I am right, the political, managerial, and technological direction of the twenty-first century, which is to automate away discretionary decision-making in the interest of perfecting rule following and rule enforcement, is a moral and social mistake.

The thinking behind legalism, however, must be given its due. Everyone, including me, plays the role of the bureaucrat who often wants and advocates for things to be more rule-governed. There is good reasoning in legalism, even if we must ultimately reject where it leads. As a result, I am not seeking to smash the regulatory state or rage against the bureaucratic machine. Instead, I want to increase both the discretionary power and the moral responsibility of the bureaucrats and their functionaries. The legalist believes that justice requires detailed and sprawling rule making, with discretion a necessary evil (since rules are imperfect). I believe that justice requires discretion, with complex rule making a necessary evil (since rulers are imperfect). We need more well-placed discretion, and we need to create ways to block bureaucracies from evolving toward an ever-increasing reliance on rules.

CHAPTER 1

AT THE CROSSROAD OF
PEACE AND FORCE

———

I T D I D N O T take long for Officer Mike to find himself in the middle of an ancient ethical dilemma. What do you do with a boy caught stealing food to feed his hungry family?

Mike was still in training when he and his partner and mentor, Officer Tom, were called to a convenience store in rural Dover Plains, New York. It was where Mike got his start policing at thirty-eight years old, not only middle age by normal standards but almost a senior citizen by the norms of policing. Mike is in his fifties today, about 6'1", and built like a retired NFL middle linebacker. He speaks like he's had years of professional broadcasting experience, able to fill time with stories and opinions he can pull at will. To this day, rural policing makes Mike nervous, because unlike cities where there is always someone within two minutes of seeing and hearing you, help can be up to forty-five minutes away on long, dark stretches of highway.

There is a dirt road off the main route that goes about a half mile up a steep hill. On top of that hill sit several old trailers, unheated, with hanging blankets taking the place of doors and windows. There is old furniture and garbage strewn around the property. The area is called Oniontown, and it has a local reputation that goes back to at least the 1940s. Everyone who lives in Oniontown is a squatter. Local lore about inbreeding and squalor has been passed down for generations. These legends lead the occasional carful of teenagers to drive up to Oniontown on drunken dares to harass the residents, engendering a longtime suspicion of outsiders in the community. Oniontown residents are said to keep large rocks, branches, and tree trunks along the hillside for throwing down onto incoming cars. They are even known to drive away police officers they do not want to see. The uneasy peace between Oniontown and the other residents is broken every decade or so by an incident of violence.

The call Officers Tom and Mike received was from a convenience store at the bottom of the Oniontown hill. When they arrived, they were faced with an irate store owner.

"The convenience store guy, rightfully, is upset," Mike recalls to me. "He wants to have the [shoplifter] arrested. He wanted to charge his bat on him."

"I want to press charges!" Mike remembers the store owner saying.

"What did he steal?" Mike asked.

It was a loaf of white bread, a jar of peanut butter, and a gallon of milk. And the shop owner knew the shoplifter, a teenage resident of Oniontown named Joey (a pseudonym).

So Mike and Tom drove up the dirt road into Oniontown, where Tom has a good reputation among the residents. Other cops, according to Oniontowners, charge onto their property looking to boss them around, barking orders and threatening arrests. Tom would take the time to listen to residents, often letting them deal with problems on their own. Oniontowners were unlikely to aim their artillery at him. The officers were let through and were soon knocking on the door of "the mayor."

"The mayor of Oniontown is a guy that is the smartest person out of all of the squatters on the mountain," explains Mike. "They give him the nicest trailer. They all go to him for assistance. If they don't understand something or they can't read or write, he helps them."

Tom and Mike informed him that Joey had been accused of shoplifting. The mayor told them to come back in half an hour. When Tom and Mike returned, a young man was sitting in the mayor's trailer with his head down.

"I know. I know," admitted Joey, "but my little brother, he hasn't eaten in weeks. What was I going to do? He's starving. He's crying, he needs food. My mother made us peanut butter sandwiches and gave us a glass of milk," Mike remembers Joey saying. "I'll go to jail. I'll go to jail," he insisted.

"Just come with us," Officer Tom responded as he thanked the mayor and escorted Joey into the back of their squad car.

The prohibition on stealing is at least as old as written law. The Code of Hammurabi, the first historical record of written law, sets the sentence for stealing as death. The book of Proverbs prohibits all stealing but explicitly mentions Joey's situation, stating that stealing a loaf of bread to feed one's family is still a sin. It puts the penalty as a return of "sevenfold" the worth of the original loaf. In Victor Hugo's *Les Misérables*, the main character Jean Valjean is sentenced to five years' hard labor for the same crime as Joey, a crime and punishment that burdens the remainder of his life. Standing opposite Valjean is a law-and-order fanatic, Inspector Javert. The law for Javert must be enforced ruthlessly, for there can be no good reasons for violating the law, no moral gray area between law and lawlessness. Javert exercises no discretion; he is a legalist. He believes in mandatory enforcement.

And so Officer Mike found himself in the middle of one of the first moral dilemmas humankind faced since they learned to write words, and therefore law. Is Mike an officer in the mold of Javert? Is he going to model himself on the book of Proverbs? Or is Mike going to do something else?

When Mike and Tom showed up at the convenience store with Joey in the backseat of their squad car, they start reasoning with the store owner.

"We said," Mike reports to me, "'[Joey] admitted to stealing the food. He said he stole peanut butter, bread, and milk. That's the same thing you told us he stole. So he's not lying to us.'"

And the store owner insisted, "So you're going to arrest him and put him in jail?"

Officer Tom replied diplomatically, "Listen, he has a brother who's four years old and he hasn't eaten in days because there's no money. He stole food to survive. Is there anything that he can do for you to pay for the items?"

"No. I want him arrested."

And Tom responded, "If you want him arrested, we can arrest him. But is there anything he can do? Can he clean up the parking lot? Can he take out the garbage? Do you need your windows cleaned? How much does bread, milk, and peanut butter cost you?"

"Three dollars and forty cents."

"We'll put him to work," said Mike. "We'll give you twice as many hours as the food costs you."

The store owner stood there thinking, hesitating.

"Have him clean up the parking lot, all the garbage and the

cigarette butts and everything. Have him clean the windows. Listen, you're going to be doing us a favor," Mike said, sensing that the store owner was softening.

The store owner relented, and the two officers, with their anti-Javertian philosophy of policing, went with the offer to Joey.

"Listen, he seems like a nice guy, he's really mad at you. You probably should have approached it a little bit differently. You could've come to us and asked, is there some way you can get food for your brother? You could've asked the store owner. Right now we have it worked out where you can clean up the parking lot and you can wash the windows, and then you go home and you get the food for free."

"For real?" asked Joey, excitedly. He jumped out of the car, got the broom from inside, and started cleaning the parking lot.

"Do we need to watch you?" Mike asked Joey.

"No, you can trust me."

Mike and Tom left, made their rounds, and drove by another couple of times that night, watching Joey hard at work as the pop-up janitor. On their final pass by the store, long after Joey had gone home, they went in to discuss the situation with the owner.

"I'm sorry," the owner said. "It's just hard when you're working so hard and someone steals from you. I want you to know that kid did such a good job that I gave him another loaf of bread and another half a gallon of milk. I made a bargain with him. I told him to come back each week. We would find something for him to do if he needed food. I'm not giving the kid cigarettes. I'm not giving him beer."

According to Mike, Joey went to work every week doing the same thing, cleaning the parking lot, cleaning the windows, and stacking the milk crates in the back for the delivery drivers to pick up. In exchange, he received bread, peanut butter, milk, and other grocery items, enough to keep his family fed.

"He probably got paid two or three dollars an hour, which isn't much, comparatively speaking, but he didn't get arrested," says Mike proudly.

In rural policing at the time Mike started, and still in a lot of rural communities today, phrases like "restorative justice" and "police reform" in response to "mass incarceration" sound like distant, urban solutions to urban problems. When I asked Mike whether he had any training in or discussion of restorative justice practices, he glanced at me quizzically as if I were asking trivia questions. He had never been trained in arbitration nor invited to talks about systemic changes to policing. Even racial issues in policing were not salient, as fewer than 1 percent of the population in Dover Plains is Black. When I explained what these things were, it turned out to be an ignorance of vocabulary, not of substantive issues. Rural policing for him always involved questions like: Do police officers need to make an arrest, or should they find a way to seek other forms of redress? Are there alternatives to jailing, and are there reasons to pursue them?

POLICE POWERS ARE ONE of the most heavily litigated domains of governmental power in the United States. Four out of the ten original constitutional amendments were about criminal justice, two about policing. An endless train of Supreme Court cases involving policing crowd the docket every term. Most litigation concerns the power police have *to do* things to citizens or what the law *authorizes*. Can they search a car without a warrant, profile a suspect based on race, or lie and deceive a suspect to get them to confess? Americans are very familiar with debates about the lengths police can go to enforce the laws.

But another, much rarer kind of litigation concerns whether to give police the power to *not* enforce the law. This I will call "selective discretion," or what is usually called the power of "selective enforcement." "The power not to enforce a law" literally means the power not *to use force* in response to a violation of law. Force includes detaining, arresting, beating, shoving, tackling, or firing a lethal or nonlethal weapon at a suspect. Other examples include a restaurant inspector who decides not to downgrade a restaurateur for spoiled meat in the fridge or an umpire who decides not to reprimand a player for cursing at him. In general, selective discretion is the power an enforcer has to look the other way when there is a violation of a rule.

Officers Mike and Tom went to extraordinary lengths to avoid the use of force. But they also displayed other values in trying to resolve a conflict rather than ignore it. Plenty of police departments ignore calls they do not deem important enough, even if laws are clearly being broken. In Los Angeles where I currently live, plenty of calls regarding loitering, illegal fireworks, petty theft, sale of items without permits, even hit and runs, are often ignored. These count as exercises of discretion. Tom and Mike on the other hand are doing something else, what philosopher and former police chief Brandon del Pozo calls "brokering," an essential feature of good policing. Tom and Mike are serving as peacemakers between conflicting parties. In addition to declining to arrest for one legal violation, they are ignoring others: minimum wage and labor laws that govern the legality of employing an underaged person, using food as compensation, for example. Hypothetically, some nosey lawyer, busybody neighbor, or Javertian legalist could file some kind of complaint about the store owner "exploiting" a hungry child for labor.

If such a person were to report the store owner, it would not be good citizenship. I would hope any relevant bureaucrat in charge would have the wisdom and discretion to look the other way. Because if not, this kind of busybody reporting might spread fear among store owners, deterring them from letting shoplifters pay for their crime with labor, insisting on arrest, and making everyone worse off. If it came to be that some authority had to put a stop to these kinds of arrangements because she did not have discretion to let it continue, then that is a flaw, not a virtue, of the bureaucratic state.

For every Tom and Mike, there is an officer who would have arrested Joey that night. At least, that is what Mike thinks. Other officers I spoke to acknowledged this about their colleagues. Many even say that at an earlier stage of their career, they would have arrested Joey. One consequence of selective discretion is that the very same situation happening in front of two different officers can result in two very different resolutions. There might be a hundred Joeys out there whose police interactions range from getting away with it to lethal force.

When I asked police officers what accounts for this wide disparity between how people are treated, they do not mention the things academics tend to look at, like bias or economic incentives. They cite age and training.

"You learn there are many ways to skin a cat," said one twenty-year police veteran to me. "The older I get, the less I arrest."

Officer Mike says, "What you see is the younger kids, they all want to arrest. You did something wrong, you're going to be arrested, because when you read the book, that's what it says. The book doesn't say 'person does this wrong, try and figure out something good for them and then work it out.'"

"When you're just starting out, you're still learning the job. You haven't seen a lot of things in the world, haven't dealt with a lot of people, so you go by the book," Officer Dave explained. "When you get to be my age, you realize there's a lot better ways to get someone to do something right," he continued, glancing over at an officer about five years into the job. The young officer nodded in agreement matter-of-factly, which led me to ask him whether he used selective discretion and if he used less of it than his older colleagues.

"Not as much, but I'm not as bad as other people [in using arrest as the only tool]," he replied. "I use it more with charging things like resisting arrest. I'm not just going to charge someone for running from me or talking back or being a dick. For me, there has to be a fight. Because I don't want to be that guy who's logging six, seven of these in a month. Then all the other guys will be thinking, what's wrong with this guy, he can't take a little lip? He's charging everyone with resisting arrest."

When I asked the same officers about whether it was good or bad that there was so much disparity in treatment, I got mostly shrugs. As they see it, it is a fact of life to get the officer you get. For that matter, you get the police department you get as you drive past different towns on a long road trip. Within the range of possible interactions, all of which are within the discretionary range of the law, there are different ways to do the same job, not better or worse ways, at least from the point of view of the police officers.

Zoom out a little bit, and you will see why political philosophers might be worried about this consequence of selective discretion. Disparity, or unequal treatment of citizens by those in power, is a defining feature of an unjust state. Disparity is also a central source of social conflict. When my neighbor gets better treatment under the law, I might bottle up this resentment until it is uncontainable, and I revolt against the state. Insofar as discretion allows the Joeys in this world to avoid jail time and a criminal record, it is good. Insofar as discretion leads to disparity, it is bad.

IT IS EASY TO SEE why Americans are preoccupied with the law of police powers, with police authority and actions. The country was founded, in part, to curb intrusive exercises of government power. But litigating police discretion is rare because it is not straightforwardly about the intrusiveness of government. Police discretion is about how best to execute the *obligations* of government. Political philosophers claim that protection of citizens from a violent threat, whether internal or external, is the primary responsibility of the state. Yet there is no constitutional right to police protection in the United States. As a result, public sentiment about discretion gets stirred only when there is a high-profile case of police *inaction*. In one prominent case that went to the Supreme Court, an abusive husband executed all his children after police failed to arrest him for violating a restraining order that his wife had reported (*Lenahan v. United States*). In another high-profile case, the local police department in Uvalde, Texas, refused to charge into a school during a mass shooting, resulting in dozens more dead children before a border patrol unit burst in and killed the shooter. In both cases, the police inactions were officially deemed cases of poor policing and unprofessional conduct. But they were neither criminal nor constitutional violations, because of police discretion.

While discretion protects police officers from legal consequences for almost every kind of inaction, there is one exception: domestic violence. As a result of well-intentioned activism, a majority of states and jurisdictions have made the use of force legally mandatory in cases of domestic violence. Police have no discretion, for they can be arrested, jailed, or fined for failing to arrest a suspect.

IN THE EARLY 1980S in Minneapolis, a young criminologist named Lawrence Sherman had a unique opportunity. When Minneapolis police were out on a domestic violence call, they typically did one of three things.

"Arrest would be one," Sherman explained, "and the other two were what they had been trained to do in the seventies, which was to try to mediate and make peace between the parties. And the third one was they would tell the offender to leave and not come back for twenty-four hours."

The Minneapolis Police Department was interested in having Sherman measure which of the three approaches most effectively prevented a person from committing domestic violence again. In this case, that meant which intervention best prevented the police from being called back to the residence for domestic violence again within six months.

Domestic violence is a common call the police get in the US. It is prevalent almost everywhere in the world. Knowing how best to respond to domestic violence is one of the most impactful pieces of knowledge a police department can have. Sherman, who became a world-renowned experimental criminologist, convinced the department that the best way to measure the effectiveness of police intervention was the same way a medical researcher approaches a new drug treatment: do a randomized clinical trial. If you can *randomly* do one of the three interventions on a domestic violence call—arrest, mediation, or separating the parties—you can see the comparative effects of each one.

It is easy to see why randomized clinical trials would be a hard sell, ethically, for measuring the effectiveness of police activity. The Minneapolis police would have to do the equivalent of rolling a three-sided die each time they received a domestic violence call. The officers would have to perform their assigned intervention on the call *regardless of what they learned or encountered on that call.* What if it was a minor call because someone punched a wall and scared the kids? If the die read "arrest," you had to arrest. What if the suspect gave a serious beating to an elderly parent? If the die read "don't arrest, only separate them," you would have to do that.

This kind of forced intervention regardless of contextual factors is essential to a randomized control trial. If a pharmaceutical company got to pick and choose which person got a drug versus a placebo based on how healthy or sick they seemed, it would completely defeat the purpose of a blind trial. Similarly, only blindly and randomly assigning a police intervention allows you to measure the effect of that intervention, as opposed to other features of the situation. The idea that you would arrest someone based on the roll of a fair die, while morally problematic, was methodologically ideal.

After months of conducting the experiment, Sherman found that, of the people who were randomly assigned "arrest," 10 percent of them were rearrested for domestic violence within six months. Of those who received mediation, it was about 18 percent. And for people who were separated for twenty-four hours, it was over 20 percent.

"So arrests worked best from the Minneapolis experiment, in

that city, in that context," concluded Sherman, and he reported these findings to the Minneapolis department.

This one little experiment on only 314 domestic violence calls in 1984 would have far-ranging policy consequences for the next forty years. The *New York Times* reported the story in their science section, and it was reprinted in over three hundred newspapers around the United States. Within a few years, twenty-eight states passed laws that made it *mandatory* for police officers to arrest someone in a domestic violence dispute, imposing a $1,000 fine or one-year prison term if they didn't do so. These "shall arrest" laws eventually expanded to include the category of violating a restraining order (or protection order) related to domestic violence. It became widespread US policy that selective discretion applied to all crimes except domestic violence.

Sherman's Minneapolis experiment took place in 1984, at a moment in political history in which the United States was eager to implement tough-on-crime policies. A member of the Reagan Justice Department called Sherman to thank him for the study and to inform him that had his study found that arrest didn't work best, they would have disputed it. It was also an era in which the feminist movement encouraged tougher policing of domestic violence, resulting in a left-right alliance on mandatory-arrest policies.

As laws evolved since 1984, a third category, "preferred arrest," emerged. "Preferred" states give officers discretion, but the official state policy is that arrest is the preferred outcome. As of 2019, mandatory-arrest states include Alaska, Arizona, Colorado, Connecticut, DC, Iowa, Kansas, Louisiana, Maine, Mississippi, Missouri, Nevada, New Jersey, New York, Ohio, Oregon, Rhode Island, South Carolina, South Dakota, Utah, Virginia, Washington, and

Wisconsin; preferred-arrest states include Arkansas, California, Massachusetts, Montana, North Dakota, and Tennessee.

This list, in fact, undercounts the places in the country that have mandatory-arrest policies, because some local police departments have mandatory-arrest policies even if their states do not.

The tidal wave of mandatory-arrest policies implemented in many US states make for a natural experiment. Over the forty years since the Minneapolis experiment, is there less domestic violence with mandatory arrest or discretionary arrest? Where is there less recidivism for domestic violence? Where is there less domestic-violence-related homicide? To count as a policy success, mandatory-arrest states need to do better than discretionary-arrest states. They should certainly not do worse. The entire justification for mandatory arrest hinges on it being a policy that reduces domestic violence and murder of spouses and helps families and cohabitants.

Unfortunately, forty years of empirical data shows that there is no difference between domestic violence rates in states with mandatory-versus discretionary-arrest policies. This is even though twice as many people are arrested for domestic violence in mandatory-arrest states than in discretionary-arrest states. In fact, almost three times as many people are arrested for domestic violence in *preferred*-arrest states than discretionary-arrest states. This is partly because states with mandatory-arrest policies result in more dual arrests: officers use far less discretion trying to determine who is at fault or the primary aggressor, so they arrest everyone in the dispute. The result is that mandatory-arrest states have two to three times more people with an arrest record, filling jails and being taken out of work and family care while the domestic violence rates remain the same.

Meanwhile, mandatory-arrest policies lead to significantly

higher murder rates of spouses. There are 35 percent fewer murders of spouses in states with discretionary- versus mandatory-arrest policies. Even outside of death by homicide, women whose partners were arrested had a much higher premature death rate than women whose partners were not. This is perhaps one of the most surprising long-term results of mandatory-arrest policies.

These findings came from none other than Lawrence Sherman, the criminologist whose Minneapolis study fueled the rise of mandatory-arrest policy. Sherman subsequently studied many other American cities in the same way, where his findings contradicted those in Minneapolis. Sometimes arrest increased domestic violence recidivism, sometimes it had no effect. The issue turned out to be complicated. Whether arrest deterred future violence or made things worse depended on a host of factors local to a community, like whether the perpetrator was employed, whether the community was affluent or impoverished, whether the household was impoverished or solidly middle class, and others. Sherman never intended the Minneapolis study to lead to a blanket policy, and his subsequent studies revealed just how ineffective and self-defeating that blanket policy was. But all of these later studies fell on deaf ears in US policy making, consistent with what the Reagan Justice Department official told Sherman back in 1984. The government wanted mandatory arrest, the evidence be damned.

Sherman's studies in these other cities allowed him to go back and see how the domestic violence victims were doing twenty-five, thirty, and forty years later. To their surprise, Sherman and colleagues found that women whose partners were arrested had a 64 percent higher premature death rate than women whose partners only received a warning.

"If you just look at African American victims, the premature death rate was twice as high. It was 5 percent if the offender had been warned, it was 10 percent if the offender had been arrested. That's the death of the victim. It's not by getting murdered. It's from heart attacks, it's from cancer," explained Sherman—that is, from illnesses and even lifestyle choices that medical research increasingly shows to be related to chronic stress. Sherman thinks that the arrest of a partner, being jointly arrested as part of a domestic violence call, becoming part of the criminal justice system, and carrying the life-long consequences of that, is traumatizing people, mostly women, and leading to their premature death.

"I think people say, 'Well, it's just an arrest, what's the big deal?'" explains Sherman, "but actually to have your partner taken out of the home in handcuffs in front of your neighbors, and to have the shame and humiliation . . . this might have been the last relationship they had, and they were more likely to be isolated, and isolation can kill through stress and other things affecting the immune system."

The racial disparity in impact arises, Sherman thinks, from the fact that Black women already live disproportionately in high-social-stress circumstances, with low-paying jobs and high demand for their labor in the home. The addition of a partner's arrest has a larger effect on them because they were already at higher risk.

IT SIMPLY ISN'T TRUE that within the range of permissible dis-cretionary acts, every act an officer chooses is as good as any other. There really are better and worse ways to do the job. And doing the job better requires knowing some background facts as well as the facts of each situation. After forty years of research, it turns out that whether arresting someone for domestic violence deters them in the future or makes things significantly worse for them and their partner depends on a great number of things. According to Sherman's research, if a perpetrator is a white male, gainfully employed, middle or upper middle class, living in an urban environment, with no previous arrest history, arrest tends to work best to prevent further occurrences. However, if the perpetrator has a history of alcohol or drug use, is unemployed, or lives in a high-poverty area, arrest tends to make things worse for both parties. If the state wants to make lives better for all victims, they will need to find alternatives to arresting partners in these circumstances.

But even these generalizations are statistical facts, not universal ones. They say things like "75 percent of employed high-earning white men arrested for domestic violence will not offend again." Statistical facts are imperfect and subject to measuring errors. But even if they were perfect, they would only tell you what is true in a majority but not all cases. To base a mandatory policy on such facts forces people to completely ignore minority cases. Maybe some affluent white guy would do better without being arrested; that is, he's in the 25 percent case who will reoffend if arrested. Similarly, maybe some non-white, unemployed person seems to be an imminent threat to his partner and should be arrested, even if evidence shows that in 70 percent of similar cases, an alternative to arrest is better. Imagine an officer knocks on a door and is faced with a domestic violence situation. Real life provides a lot more information than can ever be reckoned with in the statistical norms. Maybe there are children or elderly parents in the home. Maybe there is hunger involved or a firearm. How can this information be ignored while deciding whether this is one of the 75 percent or one of the 25 percent of exceptions to the rule? In circumstances like these, do we want officers to walk into a situation with discretion or a mandate?

THE UTOPIAN SOCIAL ENGINEER dreams that a single easy-to-follow rule, laid out in advance and executed without exception, will solve a particular social problem. The merely optimistic engineer dreams that at the very least, the rule will outperform discretion, the act of thousands of individuals making thousands of decisions based on the thousands of micro-situations they encounter. The "shall arrest" rule was a forty-year experiment about whether the complex social problem of domestic violence admits of a blanket solution. In hindsight, to think there could have been such a one-size-fits-all solution seems naïve.

CHAPTER 2

PLAYING BY THE RULES

———

O NE OF THE best cases for legalism comes from the importance of rules in ensuring fairness and equitability. Aristotle proposed the idea that living under the power of rules is far better than living under the power of people. Nowhere do we accept this more than in sports.

All sports have rules. Some of the rules define a sport. For instance, American football and rugby are different sports by virtue of their rules. In rugby, players without the ball cannot block each other. In football they can. You can pass the ball forward once per down in football, but you cannot pass the ball forward at all in rugby. These essential rules cannot be changed without changing the sport.

Other rules are there to shape the competition according to the values of those who play and watch a sport. Why is a field goal in football worth three points but a touchdown six? Because players and fans of football find touchdowns twice as valuable as field goals, maybe because getting a touchdown is roughly twice as hard as scoring a field goal. Why is there a roughing-the-kicker rule? Because a kicker is particularly valuable and vulnerable when his body is in a certain position, and players and fans dislike winning at the cost of significant risk to a kicker's body.

Rules and rule enforcement in sports exhibit the ideal of the *rule of law*. The rule of law states that rules and laws, not people, are what ought to determine proper conduct on the playing field, whether that is in sports, on the streets, or in the courtroom. Laws are made by people to reflect certain values, but once they are made in the proper way and have the proper form, they have authority in a way that people do not, even the people who made those rules. Referees and umpires cannot just decide that a particular touchdown looks four times harder than a field goal and so is worth twelve points rather than six. Rule makers cannot simply decide on new rules mid-game. Players and fans would never accept the legitimacy of a sport that did not have the rule of law. Sports wouldn't be sports if they permitted selective discretion. (Of course, sports permit other kinds of discretion, which I discuss in later chapters.)

This powerful normative drive for the rule of law in sports is the same drive for the rule of law in society. To many people, something seems fundamentally wrong with a society that allows people in charge of enforcement to bypass rules that have been instituted by legitimate rule makers. When enforcers like Officer Mike use selective discretion, the reasoning goes, they think they are preserving the spirit of the law, if not the letter, but they are mistaken. We can see why when we compare law enforcement in society with rule enforcement in sports.

It is not hard to imagine rules in sports that admit of selective discretion. Consider the "let" rule in tennis: if a serve touches the net before bouncing in the opponent's service box, it does not count; the serve must be taken over. Today the rule is enforced by way of an electronic sensor on the net cord that makes a noise and sends a signal to the chair umpire. Enforcement is mandatory; every let must be called.

Without the let rule, a serve could hit the net cord, bounce up, and simply roll slowly over into the service box, making the opponent unable to retrieve it. That kind of serve would then count as an ace, and the server would receive an easy point. If you ask players and fans of tennis what an ace is, they will say that it is a serve that is so fast or placed at such an angle or that bounces so high that a receiver is unable to return it. Hitting an ace requires a high degree of skill and execution in tennis. It is also a highly valued kind of point by fans of the sport. A point by ace is a well-earned point. The reasoning behind the let rule is that getting an ace should be a display of skill, not just a matter of luck.

The let rule is not particularly controversial, even though it is a highly imperfect rule. International tennis organizations found that most lets are, for all intents and purposes, just normal serves that only slightly graze the net. Still other lets allow plenty of time for the opponent to run up to and return the ball. Only in a small number of cases would a let serve turn into a lucky ace. Likewise, during the ordinary course of a rally, balls often hit the net cord, and then slowly bounce over onto the other side, resulting in a point. These are not considered let balls, even though these are lucky in the same way as let serves.

All of these factors render the let rule an optional, not essential, rule in tennis. All of the major professional tournaments have it, but some smaller tournaments do not. College Division I tennis does not have a let rule, and recreational players can decide among themselves whether to use or abandon it. Playing without the let rule means there will be ever so slightly more lucky aces than without, but the rule does not fundamentally transform the sport.

Yet when the let rule is in play, chair umpires or net umpires are required to enforce it—resulting in the occasional injustice to the serving or returning player. Every tennis fan can remember plenty of examples of high-stakes situations where a server hits what looks to be a clean ace or the receiving player hits an amazing return that wins the point, but the serve is called a let and the point must be played over. Such situations are not fully fair to the players, as nothing in the *spirit* of the let rule is supposed to rule out winning these kinds of points. The rule is only supposed to incentivize exciting, skillful serving.

Tennis could have, hypothetically, a rule that allows umpires to decide in circumstances such as these not to enforce the let rule. Discretion like this is easy to implement in professional tennis. The net detector can send a silent signal to the chair umpire that flashes a light, and the umpire, who is watching every single move on the court, can simply not call a let. Only if there is a lucky ace would the umpire call a let. A let rule that allowed for selective discretion would far more consistently realize the values and principles underlying the rule than enforcement without exception.

But fans and players of tennis would never let selective enforcement like this fly. The rule of law is such a powerful value in sports that all agree that it should be preserved even if the spirit of a rule is violated in the process of enforcement. The value of rule of law—with players knowing they will play under the same set of predictable rules laid out in advance—overwhelms any arguments to the contrary. Whatever injustice results from mandatory enforcement of let rules is far outweighed by the injustice of having lets be determined by a person, the umpire, rather than the rule itself.*

According to Western liberalism, the moral legitimacy of a nation-state depends a great deal on the rule of law, for the same reasons that the legitimacy of a sport depends on the rule of law. Fairness, which is an ideal of justice, requires competition and cooperation under the same set of rules, regardless of how perfect or imperfect the rules happen to be. It does not consist in allowing referees and umpires to decide, even well within the spirit of the rule, not to enforce it on a given occasion. Selective discretion is a violation of this basic value and should not be allowed.

A very different kind of case against discretionary governance comes from ancient China. Han Fei was a political philosopher thinking and writing during the Warring States period, a roughly 200-year era of constant war resulting in the conquest and unification of China under the Chin (or Qin) dynasty in 221 BCE, from which China derives its name. The *Han Feizi* is a work of political philosophy on how to govern a large-scale society of people who have been trying to kill each other for hundreds of years. It is as much a handbook of modern-day bureaucracy as anything invented in the West. Unlike the primary preoccupation of Western liberalism, which is the "input" of government—how leaders get to be leaders, how they maintain legitimacy, how they can be overthrown—the *Han Feizi* was concerned with the "output" of government, what we might call today "good governance," or the design of government: what government institutions do and how they can do what they do

---

* Many sports permit referees to make discretionary calls, like fouls or unsportsmanlike conduct, but these are different kinds of discretion, the subject of later chapters.

effectively, efficiently, and well. Western liberals most feared tyranny and arbitrariness and introduced rule of law as its constraint, while Han Fei feared the dissolution of the state and the chaos that results from having no government.

Judged on its impact, persistence, and the number of people over time who have lived under the kind of rule it advocated, the *Han Feizi* and Chinese Legalism have had far greater impact on governance than any political philosophy before and since. Only if Western liberalism lasts for another two thousand years will it give Chinese Legalism a run for its money. Never mind that it is explicitly a playbook for totalitarian governments.

Han Fei is like Machiavelli and Thomas Hobbes in that he begins with assumptions about human nature that we are supposed to take for granted in constructing a society. These assumptions are supposed to tell us how people will naturally behave if we are to force them to live together as strangers. Like Hobbes, Han Fei identifies self-interest as our defining characteristic. Faced with a choice of whether to act in their own interest or in the interest of their community, people will act for themselves. This is true both of authorities and those they govern. Leaders will no more act for the benefit of their subjects at a sacrifice to themselves than subjects will act selflessly in the interest of strangers. To make people live in a state then, and to have good governance over them, you must write laws to create punishments and rewards that align self-interest with state interests, removing decisions requiring a choice between the two. This is why almost all societies of scale have fines, jails, benefits, and bonuses. This applies to bureaucrats as well as to the people they govern.

But from here, Han Fei departs from some of his Western

counterparts. Unlike Hobbes and the even more pessimistic Machiavelli, Han Fei did not identify humans as by nature brutish, stupid, irrational, or gullible. Instead, they are *mediocre*. Whatever else he was wrong about, Han Fei was right about this. We are mediocre.

Almost all generalizations that political philosophers have made about the nature of human beings are wrong. This is as true of Han Fei's starting point as it is for Hobbes, Machiavelli, or for that matter, Aristotle or Marx. If there is anything we know about human nature in all of its history, art, literature, and the sciences, it is that traits *vary*. Graph the distribution of human beings from the number who exhibit extreme self-interest to those who exhibit extreme self-sacrifice, and you will have variation. Do the same with intelligence, rationality, brutishness, aggressiveness, or whatever feature you want, and you will find a range, with the exceptional numbering in the very few, and most of us somewhere in the middle. We are no more selfish than we are selfless, nor more brutish than we are refined. We are no more disposed to live in a large-scale society than we are inclined to live in familial tribes. We are mostly, in almost all respects that explain our behaviors and dispositions, in the middle of a spectrum. Very few behavioral or psychological traits are categorically universal to humankind, at least if the sciences are to be believed.

But this truth shows why Han Fei was on to something. Humans are not mediocre by nature, but rather, any arbitrarily chosen human being would be mediocre along most dimensions. The truly gifted exist, in athletic ability, in artistic talent, and in the wise governance of others. But as a population, we are not athletic; we are mostly in the middle, flanked by the most and least athletic. When we devise sports and games and workout routines for the masses, we would be wise to assume this. And this is also true of our cognitive traits. Are the judges in our society particularly fair, objective, or devoid of prejudice? The answer has to be: some are, some aren't, most are probably in between. So how do we organize our society in light of this truth?

Han Fei's central idea is that in a society of scale, you cannot tie all the good things you want out of good governance—well-fed people, economic development, conflict-free trade, a shared currency, resolution of conflict without violence—to something as tenuous and changeable as the quality of the people in your government. That quality will vary, converging on mediocrity.

Han Fei in his time was arguing against Confucianism, the dominant political philosophy, which begins with the assumption that any person can be cultivated to be virtuous, wise, and knowledgeable, and that society should develop such people and put them in positions of leadership. But according to Han Fei, Confucianism is not a replicable system at scale and across time. In contemporary terms, we would say that the Confucian view ignores things such as division of labor, division of knowledge, growth, turnover, and reversion to the mean. Hire the best worker and the next one will be slightly worse. Get the best manager and he will move on to better things, leaving you with the third best the next time you hire. Your best police officers represent about 10 percent of your force, your worst another 10 percent, everyone else is fair to middling.

As a result, discretion is a losing strategy for governance. Good governance by discretion requires the top percentile of people in terms of intelligence, wisdom, and moral character. Even if you end up finding such people now, you are not likely to find them again. To tie good governing to good quality people means failing—certainly in the long term, maybe even in the medium term. So we should tie good governance to something else: a system of rules, procedures, and regulation, something even the mediocre can follow.

To make governance dependent on rules, not people, Han Fei emphasized an important component of governing, the *job title*. The job title and the rule book are two sides of the same coin. Job titles are associated with detailed job descriptions, tying individuals precisely to the work they do within an organization and telling bureaucratic superiors what they are supposed to track in job evaluations. The job title and job description not only tell an employee what to do, but also what not to do, because we do not want mediocre people making decisions for which they have neither knowledge nor authority. Both kinds of failures are penalized in the job evaluation. On the other hand, staying in your lane and operating according to the rules of your lane are well rewarded.

Han Fei applied his reasoning to leadership as much as to workers, as much to kings and presidents and dictators as he did to the citizens over which they rule. People who rule and govern, make and enforce laws, are also by and large mediocre, so administering punishment and rewards to them is also a job, requiring as many strict rules and regulations as any other.

Han Fei's reasoning is familiar to anyone seeking to internationalize any kind of franchise, like for instance a restaurant chain. It is hard to imagine, but there was a time when cooking measurements, or any measurements, were not standardized. China was very early in this regard, as standard weights and measures were introduced shortly before the *Han Feizi* and, in fact, inspired Han Fei. Once you standardize measures, you can re-create food from reliable recipes. Once you standardize recipes, you can standardize food prep, service, management, and ingredient sourcing, making a restaurant franchise possible. With the same food, manual of instructions for service, and an organizational chart for management, restaurant chains can now be international, and every customer can expect and receive the same quality of food and service anywhere. Even the most mediocre employee will be able to provide service to the same standards.

Zoom out from the example of a restaurant franchise and you see a Legalist world, where we tailor rules so that even mediocre people can re-create as closely as possible the society you want them to create, no matter how large in area or population. If there are problems, the problems will be with the rules or the system, and not flaws of individuals. If a particular rule has failed us, the solution is not discretion, but finding a better rule.

Western democracy is usually held up as a stark contrast to China's authoritarianism, but at root they agree on a very significant point. Selective discretion is to be rejected. Arguments for the rule of law and for Chinese Legalism arrive at the same conclusion from very different starting points. Rules are blind but fair, and good rules of governance are the result of contemplative knowledge and foresight. Neither moral nor effective governance can depend on on-the-ground snap judgments by street-level bureaucrats. Whether in sports, in restaurants, or in government, fairness and effectiveness require that the rules need to be in charge. If the rules are good, the quality of the enforcer never matters.

Unfortunately for the Legalist, in a world where the quality of the rules is never consistent, and even the best rules face new and challenging circumstances, it turns out the quality of the enforcer matters a great deal.

CHAPTER 3

CHARGING LEFT, CHARGING RIGHT

It isn't usual for the district attorney to be called to court for a minor hearing in a minor traffic case. A DA is a boss, a CEO, the head not only of every prosecutor but of law enforcement generally in their districts. DAs oversee teams and make assignments and budgets, leaving almost all of the day-to-day prosecution to deputies. But in small-town Maine at the beginning of vacation season, sometimes the DA herself has to make arguments about routine traffic stops. So Natasha Irving is in court.

The defendant in this case was pulled over and arrested for driving while intoxicated. Another driver spotted him heading north on the highway, passing people on the shoulder. Detective John, as I will call him, received a call from dispatch and was a couple miles north of where the erratic driver was spotted. Detective John made a U-turn and drove up to an overpass to see if he could catch a glimpse of the vehicle as it approached him from below. He spotted the car described by the caller, but the driver was not speeding nor doing anything particularly erratic. He was certainly not driving on the shoulder. Detective John went ahead and pulled the driver over, administered the usual alcohol intoxication test, and sure enough the driver was over the legal limit.

In the hearing, the driver's lawyer argued that all of the evidence had to be thrown out on the grounds that the officer did not have a good enough reason to pull the car over. According to the defense, the officer stopped the driver based on hearsay. The officer did not have any direct evidence that the defendant was intoxicated or even violated any traffic law. You can't detain someone on the basis of information from someone who heard from someone that they committed a crime, the argument went, so the stop was unconstitutional. Thus all subsequent evidence collected in the case was invalid.

That morning Irving called Detective John into her office down the hall from the courtroom for a briefing. Neither seemed particularly worried. The judge in the case was the former DA. Detective John, a man in his early thirties looking uncomfortable in his "court suit," was only there to confirm the facts, which were not disputed. The two practiced some questions, the kind a detective might encounter on direct and cross examination, but both tired of the drill after about five minutes. As interesting as the question before the court that day was philosophically, the job of most courtroom argumentation is persuasion, not settling of principles. Neither Irving nor Detective John were particularly concerned about losing.

And still Irving wanted to make her case the right way. Did any court ever rule that reports from 911 dispatch can be enough evidence to pull over or detain a suspect? She found *California v. Navarette*, where the Supreme Court ruled that anonymous tips counted as acceptable evidence for reasonable suspicion. Did case law ever settle this exact question locally? She found *State of Maine v. Taylor*, which ruled that evidence acquired during routine police work can serve as justification for detaining an individual. That should be enough, thought Irving.

During the hearing, the defense lawyer, an elderly man who looked and sounded like he had been doing this kind of work for decades, questioned Detective John with an aggressive tone. No, the detective didn't have first-person evidence that the driver was intoxicated prior to the stop. No, John had not observed the defendant violate any traffic law. No, John did not speak to the caller nor ever hear a recording of the caller's report from dispatch. Without knowing the law or the case, one could conclude from the tone of the exchange that the defense had cornered a clueless cop into admitting he made an illegal stop. The defendant for his part sat fidgeting, wearing impatient exasperation on his face, but remained silent next to his lawyer.

Irving made her arguments to the judge after cross-examination, and it was over in about fifteen minutes. The judge did not seem particularly interested in the principles of evidence the defense was challenging. Even though the defense attorney essentially got the officer to admit how shaky it is, generally, to pull someone over based on hearsay, the judge ruled that, given the imminent danger, the officer did the legal thing.

That day in court was a good introduction to the difference between law and philosophy. To me, the question was worth at least an afternoon seminar's worth of discussion. Natasha Irving was herself a college philosophy major, and she understood the difference between an officer receiving a call from dispatch and an officer hearing secondhand from someone that a crime was committed. But what is that difference when it comes to generating acceptable evidence to warrant state action? Irving would be on the spot in a seminar, but in the courtroom, the issue wasn't worth a single back-and-forth between judge and prosecutor.

"I think it's a frivolous motion," Irving says. "It is the kind of motion where if it were anyone else [but me], they'd probably not make it."

"Why?" I asked. I would have thought anyone trying to fight a ticket or a jail term would use any legal means available to them and see if the argument sticks.

"It's a signal to prosecutors that you're not willing to play ball. You're just annoying them and making them do extra work. The typical prosecutor is not going to want to cut you a favorable deal if you go about endlessly filing motions like this."

The subtext, of course, is that justice is typically about seeking the best deal, not seeking the true answer to legal and moral principles. The other implication is that Irving isn't the typical prosecutor.

SIX DIFFERENT PAIRS OF shoes reside underneath Natasha Irving's desk at the Knox County Courthouse in Rockland, Maine. There were the essentials: simple black loafers for casual meetings, brown sheepskin, wool-lined boots (because this is Maine), blue running shoes sitting neatly together, still laced from the last run, and two pairs of dress shoes, one blue suede and the other white leather, like any pair you'd see a lawyer walk into court with on television shows from the nineties. Then there were the black-and-white snakeskin slip-ons for other occasions. And this was just one of her four offices.

Irving was an unlikely choice for District Attorney in mid-coast Maine, a rural area where the biggest law-and-order problems are related to alcohol and opioids. If you started driving at one edge of her jurisdiction on Highway 1 at sixty miles per hour, you would still be in it an hour later. The district is four counties wide, which means four different sheriffs from four different sheriff's offices call her the boss.

Natasha Irving ran for DA in her early thirties, after having practiced for only three years as a local defense attorney, and before that having graduated from the University of Maine law school. When I shadowed her in 2022, she had served as DA for four years, running unopposed and winning reelection later that fall. She was not only a young woman and a Democrat in a district that had only elected Republican men, she was also progressive. Canvassing for Bernie Sanders in his Democratic primary run in 2016 was what gave Irving the idea to run for elected office. A new mother at the time, Irving ran on restorative justice and criminal justice reform, words that big-city liberals used in the late 2010s to paint themselves as opponents of the mass-incarceration system that emerged out of the eighties and nineties tough-on-crime era. On paper, it was not a promising campaign.

Progressive activism against the excessive punitiveness of American criminal justice had long focused on opposing the system, not joining it. If you wanted to be a criminal justice reformer, it used to be that you represented innocent (or guilty) people on death row, you gave free legal advice to the indigent, or you were a watchdog who filed lawsuits against abusive police departments. At the very least you were a public defender, not a prosecutor. You were supposed to be the adversary in the adversarial system, not The Man. But suddenly, in the 2010s, a group of reform-minded lawyers made the simplest of utilitarian calculations. They could continue to feel good about themselves working against the system, taking donations from nonprofits, and losing nine out of ten cases trying to make a dent in the prison-industrial complex, or they could turn around and try to grab the most powerful jobs in the US criminal justice system, district attorneys, and use their power to unilaterally decide not to jail or even prosecute some of the many people who would otherwise end up populating the country's jails and prisons. Prosecutors have the widest discretionary enforcement power in the system, and the idea was to use that discretion to move in the opposite direction of where prosecutors had been headed for forty years. They would use it for less punishment and less prison time.

It was a bold idea, with many skeptics. For progressive activists, these wannabe prosecutors were sellouts, people who would inevitably be corrupted by having power and become beholden to the structural incentives toward mass incarceration, the very structures that they were trying to smash. To their tough-on-crime opponents, these mushy-hearted lawyers could never get elected. No one ever wins on a political platform of being *soft* on crime. Law-abiding citizens do the voting, the thinking went, and they will always vote for law and order.

It's a paradox of mathematics, and now social change, that sometimes you solve a hard problem by solving the even harder one, which then makes the original problem comparatively trivial. These progressive, reform-minded prosecutors started winning: Kim Gardner in St. Louis, Kim Foxx in Chicago, Larry Krasner in Philadelphia, Chesa Boudin in San Francisco, and George Gascón in Los Angeles. Progressive urban populations elected a class of progressive prosecutors and tasked them with using their vast discretion for criminal justice reform. To their critics, the Inspector Javerts of the world, progressives had hacked the system, finding in discretion a way to destroy the state from within.

Even more incredibly, one of the prosecutors elected had beaten the Republican incumbent in a red rural district in a rural state. The daughter of a beloved local boat-building teacher in mid-coast Maine, Natasha Irving took office on January 1, 2019, and made an immediate impression with her first case.

KRISTEN MCKELLAR WAS A thirty-two-year-old woman swimming in the open waters of Damariscotta Lake with a friend at dusk in August 2018, which in the Maine summers is about 8:30 pm. An active, popular, and energetic woman from an affluent family, McKeller was a writer and graphic designer, an animal lover who had rescued two bulldogs, and in every sense in the prime of her life and the life of the party. Jonathan Roberts, a Massachusetts man in his mid-forties, was out on a boat with his brother and twin daughters. He had one beer earlier in the day, which explains why his blood alcohol level would later measure .01. Roberts started driving the boat with neither headlights nor a working speedometer. McKellar saw him coming and so did her friend. Roberts claimed that he did not hear them shouting nor did he see McKellar waving her flipper at him as he approached, which at this point was twilight. According to investigators, Roberts struck and killed McKellar about 420 feet from the shore going about eighteen miles per hour.

The McKeller family wanted justice. They wanted Roberts punished. They went to the prosecutor, they went to the press, and they made a public announcement of the memorial service. The prosecutor at the time, Jonathan Liberman, was appointed by the Republican governor a year prior after the previously elected six-term DA was appointed judge. It was an election year and Liberman's opponent was Natasha Irving.

Liberman thought it was manslaughter—or that's what he wanted to signal to the public, because he took the case to a grand jury, seeking an indictment for boat manslaughter. According to the statute, the defendant had to be operating a boat with criminal negligence, acting "with gross deviation from the standard of care a reasonable or prudent person would use under the same set of circumstances." A grand jury is supposed to look at the evidence the prosecutor presents and the language of the law and decide whether the prosecutor's evidence is good enough to take the case to trial. "Good enough" here is a judgment call. It doesn't mean "enough to convict in a trial," but something like, once you give the prosecutor all the benefit of the doubt, you can see why they suspect the defendant did it. No wonder many people complain that grand juries are rubber stamps for prosecutors. That is how the rules are written. So as expected, the grand jury returned an indictment for Liberman. Then Irving defeated Liberman, and the case was hers.

Manslaughter in Maine requires a "gross deviation" from what reasonable, prudent people would do in a situation. What kind of deviations are gross? If Jonathan Roberts was on a dare from his brother to drive the boat blindfolded, that would obviously clear the bar. How about if he just happened to be glancing at his text messages at the moment Kristen was waving her flipper? That is bad, but is it a gross deviation? These are judgment calls. There is no equivalent of a Breathalyzer for measuring deviations on a scale from minor to gross, and there are no algorithms or flowcharts for how reasonable people are supposed to act in arbitrary circumstances on boats in open water. The law against manslaughter allows for a wide range of discretion.

While selective discretion is the power not to enforce a law at all, *interpretive* discretion is the power to make a judgment call about whether a law applies. Often it requires interpretations of the language of a law. Consider the basic speed law, a statute in almost every state. The basic speed law states that no one may drive faster than is safe for current road conditions. If the speed limit is fifty-five, but you are driving fifty-five during a blizzard when none of the roads are salted or plowed, you are in violation, and you may receive a ticket under the statute. A police officer or prosecutor exercises *interpretive* discretion when determining whether it is safe to drive fifty-five miles per hour during a snowstorm or other road conditions. Whether you are driving faster than is safe is in some sense a judgment call. While discretionary enforcement is the power to ignore violations of law, interpretive discretion is the power to decide whether a law is violated.

Interpretive discretion exists because laws sometimes set vague standards. Rules overall can be vague or precise. In tennis, whether a ball is in or out is a precise matter. There are lines around the court. If the ball falls outside of them, it is out. If it is inside or in any way touching a line, the ball is in. But you can also lose a point for unsportsmanlike conduct. Whether conduct counts as unsportsmanlike is vague. There is no way to measure the inappropriateness of a player's conduct to determine if it crosses a line. But prohibiting unsportsmanlike conduct is necessary. There really are on-court shenanigans that deserve a point penalty. Once, a professional tennis player took a ball out of his pocket during a live rally and let it drop in the middle of the court so he could elicit an interference call and thereby replay the point. Another time, a player threatened bodily harm to a line judge. The tennis associations long ago decided that listing examples of violations in advance would leave far too many exceptions and counterexamples, so the rule is left vague and subject to umpire discretion.

And so it goes in all institutions that have rules. Private companies, government agencies, sports, and games all have some vaguely formulated rules. The vaguer the rule, the more interpretive discretion granted to the enforcer.

When Natasha Irving looked at the boating case, she made a different judgment than her predecessor. Boats by law have to go slowly, slower than five miles per hour, when they are near the shore where it is crowded with people and other boats. Beyond 200 feet from shore, there are no speed laws for boating in Maine. Kristen McKeller was 420 feet from shore.

Irving had to make a judgment call: was Jonathan Roberts acting in a manner "grossly deviating" from how a reasonable person would drive a boat 420 feet from shore at that time of day?

"I don't know anything about driving boats," says Irving. "Seventeen, eighteen miles [an hour] doesn't sound that fast to me, but I have no earthly idea."

So Irving thought about the relevant comparison in driving. Driving eighty miles per hour in a school zone seemed grossly deviant, but forty in a twenty-five-mile-per-hour school zone seemed within the range of ordinary deviance. To her, eighteen miles per hour that far from shore, even for someone who knows nothing about boating speeds, looks a lot more like going forty than eighty in a school zone. Even if eighteen miles per hour turned out to be faster than reasonable on a lake in the dark, from what she could tell, it wasn't *grossly* outside of reason.

So was anything else about how Roberts acted grossly out of line?

The boat did not have headlights. But boats do not typically have headlights, so well within reason. Roberts drank one beer earlier in the day, also within reason.

Then there was the claim that the victim and her friend issued verbal and visual warnings that Roberts claimed not to hear. That was his word. Is it possible he heard them but drove the boat into the victim anyway? Was he doing anything grossly out of line that made him unable to hear?

It was possible. The state had no evidence either way. Without this evidence, people are free to surmise and then convince themselves, without evidence, that their guess is true. But, Irving reasoned, a prosecutor shouldn't base a case on a hypothesis without evidence. Natasha concluded that this was not a manslaughter case. It should never have gone to the grand jury. Because she was now the DA, that meant her judgment would be the government's judgment.

Informing the family was not pleasant. One month, one prosecutor tells them it is a manslaughter case, and he gets a grand jury indictment. The next month another prosecutor tells them it isn't a manslaughter case and that it should never have gone to a grand jury. From the family's perspective, the only difference was a new DA who ran on a progressive agenda. What bullshit! Whether your beloved daughter and sister is a victim of manslaughter depends on who won an election? That's not justice. That's politics. Where's the rule of law?

IN THE UNITED STATES, the power of a prosecutor is hard to overestimate. Whether you did something wrong is far less determinative of what happens to you than how a prosecutor reacts when they get your file. You may be constitutionally entitled to a trial to clear your name cleanly and completely, but if the statistics are to be believed, in about 95 percent of cases, justice is administered through plea bargaining. And the game of plea bargaining, like any kind of bargaining, is opening offers on the high and low end, in the hopes that everyone is satisfied meeting somewhere in the middle. If a prosecutor judges that justice is a three-month prison term, there's an incentive to up-charge, or charge the person with a more serious crime, or stack charges with a list of many crimes to make sure the opening offer is far higher than the final one.

Furthermore, prosecutors have other incentives to threaten more serious charges as a negotiating mechanism. DAs have a budget from the state, and trials cost money and time. They want to prevent as many trials as they can. Do you, a defendant, want to go to trial to clear your name? Then I'll take you to trial on charges with two years in prison as a minimum. Now that three-month deal isn't looking that bad. Are you going to gamble on a jury or take the deal? Barely in the equation in this process are what you've actually done, how bad it was, what real-world effect it has on people, or how your wrong might be rectified. If those facts matter anywhere, they matter to a prosecutor's discretion—how much they can live with themselves with the charges they're making.

Vague statutes and the interpretive discretion they permit are at the root of the bargaining system. The act of taking a tractor that is not yours can be interpreted as larceny (serious) or unauthorized use (not serious). One and the same act can be charged as one crime or five crimes, because vague language admits narrow and wide interpretations. All of the statutes a single act violates are fair game if you have selective and interpretive discretion.

A *Harvard Law Review* study found that as the number of charges goes up, so too does the conviction rate. If prosecutors want to get a conviction, all they need to do is charge seriously and charge numerously. They will probably get a conviction in the bargaining process, regardless of what the person did. Interpretive discretion, used in its most punitive form, works.

PROSECUTORS ARE SWORN TO seek justice in the interest of the people who elect them. Defense attorneys are supposed to advocate in the best interest of their clients. The idea is supposed to be that these adversarial interests will result in just outcomes. In reality, something is not going right. Prosecution is and has been a matter of getting wins, getting convictions, getting criminals off the street. Yet people just keep getting cycled through the system, their lives are not improving, and the public dollars spent on each person in the system is outpacing the median American's income. Prison and jail budgets keep ballooning, policing budgets are making up a third, and then half, then more than half of a city's total spending. And police departments, departments of correction, and prison-construction companies continue to argue that it is still not enough, that public safety requires even more spending on enforcement. It isn't hard to see where the country is headed. The US is turning into a country governed by crime and punishment, where public spending is increasingly viewed as the enforcement of criminal laws and the building of concrete real estate to cage its violators for years, decades, and lifetimes.

Natasha Irving and her class of progressive prosecutors ran on a platform to change all of this. No more trial penalties or charge stacking, no more prosecution of the Jonathan Robertses of the world on very serious manslaughter charges just to squeeze out pleas to lesser charges to satisfy a victim's family. Interpretive discretion would be used to move in the direction of less punishment. This new class of prosecutors was also not shy about their desire to use good old-fashioned selective discretion.

"We don't do the prosecution of drug trafficking," says Natasha Irving, meaning that she refuses to prosecute it in her district. "I want nothing to do with it. To tell you the truth, I think it's immoral."

Which is not to say such prosecution does not happen in her district. The state attorney general's office picks up where Natasha refuses to go. There is a big gap between the ordinary person's idea of a drug trafficker and the legal definition. To me, the prototypical drug trafficker is running bags of illicit drugs hidden in cases of frozen chicken parts headed to Albuquerque. In reality, the typical person charged with drug trafficking in Maine buys an extra bag of fentanyl from their supplier for a roommate. The purchaser is legally a drug trafficker under a very strict interpretation of drug-trafficking laws. Similarly, a confidential informant to me is a snitch in the cartel helping the DEA bring down a drug lord. In Maine, it is a person asked to wear a wire to capture a friend on tape agreeing to find some heroin.

"When I was in defense, I had a client who overdosed but luckily survived," Irving reflects. "The prosecution at the time could have diverted this person into treatment, but instead had them doing buys and snitching on their sellers. One, this is not helpful for somebody's recovery, and two, the people you are snitching on, I kid you not, are always your cousins up here, so you end up feeling really bad about it. My personal belief is you're not going to end the drug epidemic by putting those folks in jail or giving them criminal convictions. You're just going to make it worse. Do something to get them into treatment instead of treating them like they're some drug dealer."

The use of selective discretion gave an enormous amount of power to prosecutors during the drug wars. If you think about it, the power not to charge someone doesn't just mean you have the power to be nice. It also means the power to dangle a charge over a person. Do what we ask and you go free, no record. Fail to agree and we'll do what we're supposed to do by law anyhow. A cop or prosecutor can ask you to do just about anything in exchange for ignoring the charge, and the range of things law enforcement has had people do has been particularly abhorrent. But progressive prosecutors noticed that discretion is a two-edged sword, useful for the interests of law enforcement at the expense of defendants, or useful for the interests of defendants, full stop. Just as prosecutors can dangle a charge in exchange for favors, they can threaten a charge in order to divert a person to treatment, dangling it over them until they complete treatment. A progressive prosecutor can unilaterally issue restorative rather than punitive justice. The most widely shared platform for progressive prosecutors is the refusal to do confidential informant deals for reduced charges, removing threats of long-term incarceration for drug possession and distribution crimes, and finally in some cases like Irving's, the outright refusal to charge such crimes.

THE BACKLASH TO PROGRESSIVE prosecution was swift and fierce. Almost as soon as progressive prosecutors won, all manner of police blowback started. Police started refusing to cooperate with prosecutors on cases. They went out on calls and refused to intervene, telling victims or bystanders to take their grievances to the progressive DA, who, they said, was refusing to enforce the law.

"I had a sheriff's deputy in one of my counties who pulled somebody over for erratic driving," Irving tells me. "He had said to the people in the car that the idiot DA is not charging OUI (operating under the influence) anymore, and then started talking shit about me."

The only way Irving knows about this incident, and not about probably dozens more like it, is that an old family friend happened to be in the car at the time. Irving had the sheriff pull the video of the stop, and sure enough, there was the deputy saying exactly what was reported.

Kim Gardner of St. Louis received some of the highest-profile police blowback, extensively reported by ProPublica. When she refused to prosecute daycare workers for having toddlers put on Incredible Hulk mitts and box each other, the police union called for her ouster, claiming she was a promoter of "Toddler Fight Club." One detective refused to testify in nine of his own murder cases because of disagreements with Gardner, leading to acquittals. Gardner stepped down in 2022.

A popular Chicago police blog referred to the newly elected Black prosecutor, Kim Foxx, as "Crimesha." Chesa Boudin of San Francisco, elected in 2019, was recalled in a 2022 vote. And back in mid-coast Maine, Natasha Irving made a single discretionary call that resulted in a similar kind of police blowback.

"There was a traffic accident that resulted in a death. And the person who died was the addiction counselor who had worked for the sheriff. Beloved."

Irving studied the report. In her judgment, it was an accident. The other driver just didn't see the car coming as he pulled out too early on a foggy morning. But he did have a criminal history, an older one; he had been clean for a decade. No alcohol and no drugs were involved in the case.

"The sheriff's department was pissed. I mean, beyond pissed at us for not prosecuting," Irving claims.

In another era, if a prosecutor wanted to prosecute to appease the sheriff, to appease the family, to appease the public, they could and would prosecute, even if they couldn't get a trial conviction. They'd likely get some plea deal out of it. They might lose a trial but get PR points. All of these were perks of the job, a way of using your discretion for some other aim. But Irving refused. Then one day, her office needed the sheriff's office to serve a summons for a different case. The office refused.

Why should they, when Irving wasn't prosecuting who they wanted prosecuted, they explicitly told her.

"Progressive prosecutors are social justice warriors masquerading as law enforcement," claimed police union blogs, fraternal orders' press releases, and opinion sections in local newspapers. It is "politicking in the guise of prosecution," wrote one critic. In reality, the issue is subtler. The issue is what attitudes, principles, or philosophies are supposed to ground decision-making when it comes to interpretive and selective discretion. If it is bad to refuse to prosecute someone for drug trafficking because you think it makes the community worse off, is it good to prosecute to appease a sheriff's department that you depend on for law enforcement? If progressive prosecution is politicking, is its alternative politically neutral?

Ronnie Goldy was a traditional tough-on-crime, tough-on-drugs conservative and served as a Kentucky commonwealth's attorney, their title for a DA, from 2017 to 2020. The opioid epidemic hit Kentucky hard in the late 2010s, continuing right on through to the time of this writing. People were overdosing and dying alone, sometimes because other people they were doing drugs with, friends and maybe dealers, were not calling 911 to save them, out of fear that they themselves would be arrested on drug charges when police and medics arrived. Kentucky decided to deal with this one tragic aspect of the opioid epidemic by passing the Good Samaritan law, making callers like this immune from prosecution on such charges.

Ronnie Goldy noticed that the law made Good Samaritans immune only from charges of drug and drug paraphernalia possession. So he found three Good Samaritans, opioid users who called 911 to save a friend, and instead charged them with wanton endangerment, ten counts for each Samaritan. When reporters Matt Kielty and Peter Andrey Smith from WNYC's *Radiolab* pointed out to Goldy that such charges contradicted the entire justification for passing the Good Samaritan law, Goldy replied:

> Sure, I get it. And I totally understand it. I totally understand the reason behind it. But what I may think morally or personally, I don't have that luxury. I have a statute that I have to follow because when I took the oath of office I said I would uphold the laws of the commonwealth. And if it's a crime, it's a crime. I don't get to say, "Well, but they were trying to do the right thing." If it's a crime, it's a crime, and I have to pursue it.

There is no more overused but false cover for a cop or prosecutor to hide behind when trying to explain a blatantly wrong, controversial, or unpopular decision than to say that they were "simply following the law." There is no such thing for cops and prosecutors as simply following the law when the law not only permits, but requires, discretion. No one with selective and interpretive discretion passively follows the law. There is always a choice of which laws (or which interpretations of the laws) to follow and which ones to ignore.

A more honest answer in Goldy's case would be that he thinks the Good Samaritan laws allow drug users, who are a disgusting and immoral blight on our society, to get away with something they shouldn't get away with. Maybe Goldy is like *Les Misérables*'s Javert and thinks every wrongdoer ought to be punished. Faced with a conflict between two laws, a law that criminalizes doing drugs with people and a law that aims to decriminalize it to save more lives, Goldy is choosing the path of punishment. Whatever his reasons, they are driven by a moral or political conception of drug-use crimes, the proper punishment for them, and the role of the prosecutor in selectively executing laws passed by the legislature. Goldy isn't simply following the law any more than a prosecutor who ignores the wanton endangerment law in order to uphold the spirit of the Good Samaritan law.

It isn't only the law, but prosecutors' moral, political, and pragmatic principles that determine their decisions to charge someone with a crime, every time. With discretionary power comes moral responsibility. The laws are not mere instruments; they are tools in the hands of people. As it goes for prosecutors, so it goes for all people with discretionary power, selective and interpretive, no matter where it is held. This fact leads us to a question we should answer for ourselves as people who elect, live with, and are affected by these decisions: what are the principles such people ought to follow when using their discretion?

When Natasha Irving and her predecessor Jonathan Liberman had to make a choice about whether Jonathan Roberts operated his boat in a grossly deviant way, on what basis should they make that choice? Is it right for prosecutors to use their discretion in a way that is favorable to their reelection? Is it okay for them to appease the sheriff's department that they rely on for law enforcement? Is it okay for them to appease a victim's family? How about making prosecution decisions to prevent the spread of a virus?

When COVID-19 first hit in spring of 2020, police departments and prosecutors suddenly had to balance locking someone up with increasing the risk of COVID spread at the local jail. All public health and governmental officials said, "use more discretion." What they really meant was raise your standards for arresting and jailing people. Suddenly, containing an airborne virus was supposed to determine prosecutorial discretion. Was that right?

Every one of these considerations are *extra-legal reasons* to enforce or not enforce a law, or to interpret the law one way rather than another. If you answer yes to some but not to others, you are advocating a principle by which you think extra-legal reasons can and should be used to govern discretion. Maybe you think prosecutors should never consider their own reelections but should consider the spread of a virus. Maybe you think they shouldn't appease sheriffs but should be sensitive to victims and their families. No matter what principle you formulate, you are not being morally and politically neutral. The police departments bitterly opposed to working under progressive prosecutors seem to want prosecutorial decision-making to be deferential to the interests of police. This stance is no more apolitical, neutral, and objective than the stance against prosecuting low-level drug offenses, which is more deferential to the interests of drug users and their families. If a police department wants to implement the principle "interpret a vague statute so that as many acts as possible count as being a crime," that is no less political than its opposite, "interpret a vague statute so that it excludes as many acts as possible."

All of this means that it is unavoidable for us to ask and answer substantive questions about how selective and interpretive discretion ought to be applied or the right and wrong ways to use it. We are voting for the people doing the charging. We might very well be the people who will be charged. Nobody who claims to just follow the law is worth your time. In hard and vague cases and in hard questions of conflicting public policy and public interests, there is no such thing.

NEIGHBORING NATASHA IRVING'S DISTRICT in mid-coast Maine is District 3, home to the cities of Lewiston and Auburn. District 3 differs from Irving's in that its population is a little larger on account of its cities being larger. District 3 also differs in that the Lewiston police department and the DA's office have always been more aligned: if the police made an arrest, the DA charged. This is not a district where the DA disagrees with the police and not a district where the police believe in less enforcement. By 2023, the backlog in criminal cases in District 3 was 5,200 cases, about four years long. The jail was overflowing. When the former DA was appointed judge, the deputy DA stepped into the position and resigned three weeks later. In an unprecedented rebuke, a judge publicly criticized the DA's office for the backlog. District 3 went through four DAs in two years. There is no evidence of a crime wave overtaking District 3, but the criminal justice system there is nonetheless falling apart.

Also in 2022, Natasha Irving was reelected to a second term. She ran unopposed.

CHAPTER 4

THE LAWS OF BUREAUDYNAMICS

——

I FOUND MYSELF IN the position of being both rule maker and enforcer recently. A few years ago, I took up a job overseeing a series of essay prizes in philosophy. The prizes were set up before my time in order to help reward excellent papers by early career scholars. The idea was that it is difficult climbing the ladder to be a successful academic. Why not help graduate students and recent PhDs where they can submit papers they are already writing, and if the paper stands out to a committee of distinguished senior philosophers, they will get a $5,000 prize, have the paper published in a distinguished journal, and get to brag about winning a named essay prize on their CV? Maybe the prize will secure them a job or promotion, or at the very least their paper will become the object of attention for a while.

About a decade into the prize series, I received a question from one of the prize administrators. Someone wanted to know our policy regarding people who had spent time away from academia to raise children and then came back. Would they be able to submit an essay? The rule for submission read as follows: "authors must have been awarded their PhD within fifteen years of the submission date for the prize." The prize administrators were all philosophers more distinguished and experienced than me, but since I was in charge, it was up to me to respond.

Institutions started incorporating parental leave policies around 1993. The principles behind parental leave are about recognizing the value of familial caretaking in a society that does not treat it as compensated work and even penalizes it in career advancement. And what could be more beneficial, even necessary, for the persistence of a society than good child-rearing? But these very noble principles lead to policy puzzles. What about parental leave for men or for non-birthing spouses in general? Is there extra parental leave for single parents, who have it at least twice as hard? Things get even more complex as exceptions mount. What about family members who need care but who aren't children? What about children with disabilities or for that matter other family members who require more at-home care? What about time for individuals who have to care for themselves due to medical circumstances? I started thinking that I should ask the person who wrote to us about her life circumstances, but that was going to open up a procedural rabbit hole. How many additional years would we grant for raising a child? What if they raised two or three children? And what kind of verification method would we use to make sure people are honest about their claims to being an exception to the rule?

In the end, I refused to engage in policymaking. My decision was that we should let the person know the spirit of our essay prize. We were giving awards to early career scholars because they could reap better rewards from these prizes than established senior scholars. If in their own judgment, given the totality of their life circumstances, authors considered themselves early-career scholars, they could submit. We would not have an explicit policy either way. The prize administrator, a distinguished philosopher and experienced higher education administrator, agreed with me.

Larger institutions, with employment law, recruitment, and reputations at stake, do not feel like they have the luxury of exercising discretionary judgment against complex rule making in this way. School districts, one of the professions that employs the largest number of women in the economy as a whole, can have extremely baroque policies for parental leave. I know of one district that has different leave policies depending on whether births are natural or by caesarean and requires medical documentation as proof. Anyone with a little experience can immediately see the major problems with such a policy. What about other complications from natural birth, comparable to the trauma of caesareans? But in addition to all of its shortcomings for the people it serves, there are stacks of exceptions and contingencies that the policy does not cover. What about men who are primary caretakers of children, who have neither natural nor caesarean births? I personally know two men whose wives died during childbirth. Would they be covered if they worked for this school district? What about leave policies for parents who adopt children?

The spirit or principle behind rules is always very general so as to be easily accepted by consensus: prizes are for early career scholars, childcare is valuable. But the details of implementation require specific decisions about atypical cases, like a single father who just adopted a child. The regulatory rabbit hole of rule making is how to balance the spirit of the rule with its concrete implementation in the face of non-exemplary or atypical cases.

The choice for rule makers is between policies so detailed and specific they cover every last special case or vague policies that leave interpretive discretion up to enforcers. Some companies have a "generous" parental leave policy and leave it at that. Others, like the state of California, have tables and flowcharts, hoping to cover every contingency. What rule makers end up with is more the result of practical than philosophical considerations. Perhaps a firm is only concerned with how to compete for employees against other firms. Others might be fearful that if they leave implementation up to a manager and the manager makes a bad call, they will face a lawsuit for gender discrimination.

There's a very natural evolution in administering rules in an organization, small to large, such that, over time, rules and their administration only become longer and more complex, never shorter and simpler. If there were laws of nature for bureaucracies, this would be my choice for law #1, the first law of bureaudynamics.

LAW #1: RULES AND THEIR ADMINISTRATION INCREASE IN COMPLEXITY OVER TIME.

The first law of bureaudynamics does not only apply to corporations or governments. We are susceptible to it even in the most mundane of circumstances. When my daughter was about seven, we started to assign her chores at home so she could learn responsibility and contribute to family life. Because she was so young, not many chores were appropriate for her to do, so we decided she could empty the dishwasher after the completion of a wash cycle. At first, life with responsibilities was new and exciting. But pretty soon it turned into, well, a chore. Getting her to do it in a timely way became a fight.

We started compensating her with an allowance. We'd let the dishes stack up in the sink to give her a visual reminder of what happens when she fails at her job. But sometimes I just did the chore myself because I was tired of all the dirty dishes in the sink.

The rule in the house started as "Darcy empties the dishwasher when the dishes are clean." Then it became "Darcy empties the dishwasher when the dishes are clean and will receive $2 for every load." After the task still went undone a couple of times, we told her she would not receive the allowance if it were not done in a timely manner. Arguments started about what counted as timely. The dishwasher takes a couple of hours to complete a cycle, she rightly pointed out. How much time after it is completed does she have to put the dishes away? The dishes are pretty hot at the end of a cycle, she again rightly observed. Plus, we often run it overnight, and she has school in the morning. Why can't she complete the job after school?

By then, the rule had morphed into "Darcy empties the dishwasher when the dishes are clean, within 2 hours of completion of a cycle, unless it is done overnight, in which case she has until after school to complete the job."

After a few more failures, she argued that she had obligations after school, like homework or lessons. When I said the chore had to be done by evening, she rightly pointed out that sometimes she has Girl Scout meetings in the evening.

That was not all. She started getting into the habit of opening the dishwasher, unloading maybe a few dishes or silverware, and then getting distracted with some other project, leaving the dishwasher open and the dishes unemptied, sometimes for hours. She pointed out, again correctly, that nothing in the rules said anything about how long she had to take to complete the task once she started. For a while, I turned on the song "American Pie" by Don McLean as a kind of timer. She had to finish it by the end of the song, which I thought was reasonable at eight minutes, forty-two seconds. So the proper rule evolved to be:

> Darcy empties the dishwasher, for a $2 allowance, when the dishes are clean, within 2 hours of completion of a cycle, unless the cycle is run overnight, in which case she has until after school to complete the job, unless there is something scheduled, in which case she has until bedtime, and she must complete the task within 8 minutes 42 seconds of beginning it, or she does not receive $2.

This is one rule in one household governing a single individual. Scale this up to an organization with fifty or fifty million people, and it is no wonder rules and laws balloon in length.

The first law of bureaudynamics is essential in paving the road to legalism. It stems from the ideals of the rule of law. Fairness requires that rules need to fully inform the people about what compliance requires. Philosophers of law call this the guidance value of law. Living in a neighborhood, living in a household, or working in a society may not be a natural thing for everyone, especially if the neighborhood has streets, vehicles, sidewalks, businesses, lots of people, and economic transactions. Rules are supposed to tell us how to live harmoniously among others and avoid penalties from enforcers. It is a doctrine of liberalism that citizens cannot justly be a victim of state violence like arrest, imprisonment, or execution without knowing exactly what rules of the state they have broken. If I am to dock my child two dollars of pay per week, she is entitled to know exactly why. In this case, she can see which of the many instructions she failed to follow.

The rule of law also requires that enforcers be given sufficient instruction on when a law is violated. Philosophers of law call this the process value of law. Laws against drunk driving, for example, date back to 1906, almost fifty years prior to the invention of the Breathalyzer. It was not easy for enforcers to know how to fairly and accurately pick up people who were too drunk to drive. Police had to rely on their own judgment. They would administer various tests like smelling a driver's breath, having them walk on a painted line, and so forth—tests that some continue to use to this day. But none of these tests are written in law itself. The law had little guidance value for telling people exactly how much alcohol was safe to consume and little process value for enforcers. Today US law states that a specific blood alcohol level, usually .08 percent, is sufficient to charge an individual with driving under the influence of alcohol. Formal Breathalyzer, urine, or blood alcohol tests, with their measurable accuracy rates, make such charges decisive. The law now has very good process value. The guidance value of drunk-driving laws, on the other hand, isn't as good. Few people travel with reliable Breathalyzers. Instead, citizens have to rely for guidance on imperfect rules of thumb like "no more than one drink an hour." Even so, the process value of the law is so precise and devoid of discretion that it is worth having despite its poor guidance value.

Laws usually need to increase in complexity to achieve good process value. The drunk-driving example is the exception rather than the norm. Consider noise ordinances. The noise regulations in West Covina, California, are 2,200 words long consisting of fourteen subsections, determining the appropriate noise levels at all hours of the day for all manner of activities: parties, construction work, barking dogs, even television volume. One sample subsection looks like this:

> It shall be unlawful for any person within any residential area of the city to repair, rebuild, or test any motor vehicle upon private property in such manner as to create any noise which causes the noise level at the property line to exceed the ambient noise level by more than five (5) decibels.

This law has very poor guidance value but good process value. The typical citizen does not own a decibel meter and does not know that decibel scales are logarithmic so as to understand a five-decibel difference. The typical complainant probably cannot tell you where a violator's property line is. But any police officer carrying a decibel meter can show a violator right away why they are receiving a citation.

WHILE BOTH GUIDANCE AND process value explain some of the complexity of laws and rules, the most important driver of the first law of bureaudynamics is *mistrust*. Most complex rules arise because people do not trust each other with the discretion to interpret them correctly. Give someone an inch of interpretive discretion, and they'll take a mile. Nowhere do you more clearly see mistrust manifest into byzantine rules than in the US tax code.

Consider just one small section of the code, concerning what money I earn from this book ends up being taxable income. Any payment from the publisher, the great team at Norton, is earned income. But what about the prize money that will undoubtedly rain down on me after publication from all the acclaimed literary awards I will receive? Here is the relevant language in the US tax code:

Gross income does not include amounts received as prizes and awards made primarily in recognition of religious, charitable, scientific, educational, artistic, literary, or civic achievement, but only if

(1) the recipient was selected without any action on his part to enter the contest or proceeding;

(2) the recipient is not required to render substantial future services as a condition to receiving the prize or award; and

(3) the prize or award is transferred by the payor to a governmental unit or organization described in paragraph (1) or (2) of section 170(c) pursuant to a designation made by the recipient.

What I like about this rule is that it is very easy to imagine the story of its origin . Rules and regulations can be incredible repositories of their own histories. If I had to guess, the rule evolved because Congress decided that awards like the Nobel Prize should be tax exempt. Maybe an idealistic congressperson argued that we need to use the tax system to incentivize excellent people to do excellent things. Then someone, maybe a scientist, auditioned and became a contestant on *Jeopardy!*, won a substantial amount of money, claimed it as an award for scientific achievement, and Congress could not collect taxes on it.

Shortly thereafter, a bright young person entered something like a talent pageant to compete for a substantial prize and won. The winner, like winners of beauty pageants, toured with the promoting company, bringing in earnings through appearances.

In light of these two cases, some federal bureaucrat then figured that using your knowledge to win money on a game show is not something the government needs to incentivize. Hence, clause (1) was born. Some other federal bureaucrat figured that talent-pageant touring looks more like earning money from a company than it does like winning a Nobel prize, so clause (2) was born. What better way to remember the loopholes we've seen exploited than to write them into the rules themselves?

Enforcers of the tax code presume and expect that taxpayers will lie, fight, deny, or exploit every loophole to get away with paying the least amount possible. Taxpayers presume and expect that the government will do everything in its favor to collect as much as possible. These are relationships of antagonism and mistrust, not cooperation.

What is true of taxes is true of just about all rule-making schemes. The more mistrust, the more rule makers will expect the devious citizen to look for loopholes and exceptions to the rule and anticipate them, turning a rule into pages of subsections and clauses. Legislation, a saying goes, is aimed at the dumbest or most devious among us.

Similarly, the mistrustful citizen reasons that enforcers will be tyrants, exercising unreasonable power over them unless the rules prohibit it. This is why citizens, not enforcers, tend to push for high process-value rules. Given a choice, they will refuse to accept any tax law with the clause "or other similar cases" or any laws that give interpretive discretion.

To the mistrustful rule maker, any interpretive discretion given to subjects is an invitation for exploitation. To the mistrustful subject, interpretive discretion granted to enforcers is an invitation to tyranny. Both will push for more precise and complex laws to close off these possibilities.

This brings us to the second law of bureaudynamics, which arises because of mistrust.

LAW #2: PRESSURES TO REMOVE DISCRETION IN RULE MAKING ARE FAR GREATER THAN PRESSURES TO GRANT IT.

In 1983 Edward C. Lawson, a tall Black man with long dreadlocks, was a young civil rights activist. His appearance was enough to get him stopped, questioned, and arrested fifteen times in eighteen months while walking around an affluent area of San Diego, California. Each time, Lawson was charged, not with doing anything wrong, but of failing to provide "credible and reliable" identification to the police officer who requested it. According to a California statute at the time, police officers had a right to request such ID from people who "loiter or wander on the streets" and to demand that a person or their ID carries "a reasonable assurance" of the ID's authenticity. If you think hard enough about it, as Edward Lawson did, this was one of those laws that allowed police officers to stop anyone on the street and arrest them, regardless of what they were doing or what kind of ID they had. Birth certificates, driver's licenses, passports can all be faked. If an officer says they suspect some ID is fake, what kind of "assurance of authenticity" might Lawson provide that can't also be suspected of being fake? Lawson concluded that the reason he was arrested fifteen times had nothing to do with his ID since fourteen of those charges were dropped. The law was only a pretext. He was arrested for walking while Black.

Because the vagueness of laws gives rise to discretion, there will inevitably be good uses and bad uses of it. Sometimes the judgments are so bad and so frequent that they result in blatant violations of someone's basic human rights. Lawson, representing himself, argued his case all the way to the US Supreme Court. There he was forced to hand the case over to a lawyer for the ACLU, who helped him win a 7–2 decision. The Supreme Court voided the California statute, not for violating Lawson's civil rights under the equal protection clause, but for vagueness.

"Void for vagueness" is a doctrine the Supreme Court has practiced since 1926. Whether a law is too vague depends on two tests. The first is whether an ordinary, reasonable person can understand how to comply with the law in various circumstances. This is a guidance value test. A law without sufficient guidance value, the reasoning goes, should not be a law. The second test is whether the law encourages *arbitrary and discriminatory* enforcement. This is a process value test. A law on the books with absolutely no process value is one that encourages, or at least permits, arbitrary and discriminatory enforcement. Justice Sandra Day O'Connor, writing for the majority, stated that the California statute failed both. No citizen can learn from the law what they could possibly carry that guaranteed they were not targets of enforcement. And if officers were intent on arresting Lawson for arbitrary reasons, like they didn't like his attitude, his race, or had some kind of quota to fill, the law gave cover. Laws are allowed to be vague, but this one was too vague for the Burger Court in 1983.

Unlike Han Fei who most feared the dissolution of the state due to bad governance, Western political philosophers seem to most fear arbitrariness. John Locke, the revered Enlightenment philosopher considered a father of liberalism, decried governments that rule by "extemporary Arbitrary Decrees." The French jurist and political philosopher known as Montesquieu noted that laws that are too simple and vague are an instrument of despotism by permitting arbitrariness. Even Machiavelli, whose *The Prince* is most remembered as an advice column for strongmen dictators, argued that within states, "citizens are protected by the rule of law from arbitrary domination." In Western philosophy, arbitrariness is not bad because it is ineffective, inefficient, or mediocre. It is *wrong*. It is *unfair*. It is *unjust*. It needs to be held in check by the rule of law.

Arbitrariness, though, is not easy to define. Sometimes it is equated with despotism, but all despots are not the same. An enlightened despot—someone who makes the right decisions for the right reasons—is still a despot, according to Western liberalism. But an enlightened despot's decisions are not arbitrary. They are, hypothetically, done for the right reasons.

Some definitions of arbitrariness state that judgments made by people, that is, discretion, are by definition arbitrary, since they are not judgments forced on us by rules or laws. This too is a mistake. Even in sports, the exemplar of rule of law, there are discretionary matters like unsportsmanlike conduct, for which there are no precise rules and very little process value. Unsportsmanlike-conduct calls are entirely discretionary, but they are not *thereby* arbitrary. There are good calls and bad calls. Some calls might be arbitrary, but the fact that they are judgment calls does not make them all arbitrary. Referees can have very good, even decisive, reasons for making an unsportsmanlike-conduct call, or they can have bad or no reasons.

When people are worried about authorities exercising arbitrary authority, they have two paradigm cases in mind. One is when decisions look truly random. One kind of objectionable arbitrary enforcer is the referee who, without rhyme or reason, treats one player's conduct as being fine but the same conduct as bad when another player does it. This is usually what is meant when people complain about rules being enforced according to the whims of an authority.

Corrupt enforcement is the second kind of arbitrary authority people complain about, even though it is neither random nor based on whims. This paradigm of arbitrariness is when a referee takes a bribe or wants revenge on a player and therefore issues a penalty. In cases of corruption, referees have reasons for their calls, but they are simply unacceptable reasons.

Racially biased enforcement counts as an example of corruption. It is making a decision for bad reasons, not no reason at all. This is why we are so enraged with cases like Edward Lawson's. The central normative truth we want enforcers to respect is to *treat like cases alike, and unalike cases unalike, for the right reasons.* If a Black Ed Lawson poses no more threat to pedestrians than a white Ed Smith, and enforcers do not stop and arrest Ed Smith, then stopping and arresting Ed Lawson must be done for the right kind of reason. Whether they stop Ed Lawson on a whim or due to prejudice, they are exercising a kind of impermissible arbitrary power. Disparity in treatment is not in itself the problem. Disparity without appropriate normative difference is. This is the arbitrariness of enforcement from which we need protection and why we need the void-for-vagueness doctrine.

Removing void for vagueness because of mistrust of law enforcement is one instance of how the second law of bureaudynamics drives us toward legalism. It is also an instance of how the second law helps to explain the first. Vague laws must be replaced with precise ones, and precise ones have to be longer and more complex. The path seems inevitable as long as mistrust is taken for granted. But void for vagueness is not the first instance we've seen of the second law. Mandatory-arrest policies arose precisely because rule makers wanted to take discretion away from police officers, believing they could not be trusted to make smart judgments about who to arrest in domestic violence cases. Forty years of a failed policy have still not led to the restoration of that discretion.

IS THERE ANY VAGUE law that is safe from the laws of bureaudynamics? On the open highways in Montana, the basic speed law used to be the only speed law. This is the law that one is never to drive faster than is safe given the road conditions at the time. Montana essentially told its citizens and its highway patrol officers to use their best judgment as to a safe, reasonable, and prudent speed. Speed laws were not byzantine and therefore gave both citizens and enforcers a high degree of interpretive discretion. It is still law in most US states.

But in Montana on March 10, 1996, Highway Patrol Officer Kenneth Breidenbach saw a brand-new Chevrolet Camaro speed past him on Highway 200. It was eight in the morning with extremely light traffic and very good visibility. The road was dry but narrow, with no shoulders, and twists and turns going up a mountain marked by occasional frost. Breidenbach sped forward to match the speed of the car and employed the three-second rule, which is to maintain a time-distance of three seconds between the patrol car and the pursued car. Breidenbach followed the vehicle for eight miles, clocking it at a consistent eighty-five miles per hour.

Once they reached a shoulder, Breidenbach pulled over and issued a ticket to Rudolph "Butch" Stanko, a local meat packer. Stanko had, and would continue to have, a very colorful history sticking middle fingers to the government. A heavyweight wrestling champion in his youth and a weightlifting record holder in his sixties, Stanko had been convicted of violating federal meat-packing laws in the 1980s and received multiple speeding tickets for driving in excess of 124 miles per hour, for which he refused to pay the fines. Stanko had not, at this point, gotten into any traffic accidents. For this ticket, Stanko's refusal to pay resulted in an arrest, a trial, and a conviction, which he appealed to the Montana Supreme Court, seeking to void the basic speed law for vagueness.

In testimony to the court, neither Breidenbach nor the attorney general could directly say what they thought was a safe, prudent speed on that day in those conditions. But they insisted that eighty-five was unsafe.

It was not a good look for the state. The government looked as though it did not know its own criteria for applying the law and couldn't draw the line between safe and unsafe speeds. But this is not unreasonable when it comes to vague standards. A classic exercise in philosophy classes has students say how much of a person's head has to be devoid of hair for them to count as bald. It is impossible to give an answer. Yet it is quite easy for everyone to accurately point to a picture of a bald man. That is how vagueness works.

Stanko for his part cited the handling properties of his brand-new Camaro, the width of the tires, and his own skills as a driver. He was evidently quite persuasive. Montanans are quite sensitive to how steady and in control very powerful American muscle cars feel at eighty-five miles per hour.

It was a close ruling, four to three, but Stanko emerged victorious. The Montana Supreme Court voided the basic speed law for vagueness. The reasoning was no different from how the US Supreme Court had previously ruled on other vague laws. The basic speed law, they reasoned, left it to one of the 190 highway patrol officers to decide whether someone had violated the law in a way that ordinary citizens are not able to know whether they had violated the law in a given circumstance. That opened the door to arbitrary and discriminatory enforcement.

In response to the ruling, Montana imposed maximum speed laws, precise ones, to replace the single vague basic speed law. As of 2023, they are

> (1) . . . the speed limit for vehicles traveling:
> (a) on an interstate highway outside an urbanized area of 50,000 population or more is 80 miles an hour at all times and the speed limit for vehicles traveling on interstate highways within an urbanized area of 50,000 population or more is 65 miles an hour at all times;
> (b) on any other public highway of this state is 70 miles an hour during the daytime and 65 miles an hour during the nighttime;
> (c) in an urban district is 25 miles an hour.
> (2) A vehicle subject to the speed limits imposed in subsection (1) may exceed the speed limits imposed in subsection (1) by 10 miles an hour in order to overtake and pass a vehicle and return safely to the right-hand lane under the following circumstances:
> (a) while traveling on a two-lane road; and
> (b) in a designated passing zone.
> (3) Subject to the maximum speed limits set forth in subsection (1), a person shall operate a vehicle in a careful and prudent manner and at a reduced rate of speed no greater

than is reasonable and prudent under the conditions exist-
ing at the point of operation, taking into account the
amount and character of traffic, visibility, weather, and
roadway conditions.

(4) Except when a special hazard exists that requires lower
speed for compliance with subsection (3), the limits speci-
fied in this section are the maximum lawful speeds allowed.

(5) "Daytime" means from one-half hour before sunrise
to one-half hour after sunset. "Nighttime" means at any
other hour.

It was a pyrrhic victory for Rudy Stanko. Montana speed laws are
now *more* restrictive than they used to be, and Stanko's kind of driving is now *clearly* rather than vaguely outlawed. But a bigger slap in
the face is that Montana law still employs a basic speed law in clause
(3). As a result, no powers were taken away from police officers for
arbitrary enforcement. But this new byzantine speed law passes the
guidance value test. An ordinary person knows exactly when they
are violating the law: when their speedometer goes over eighty in
very specific circumstances, seventy in others, sixty-five in others,
and twenty-five in others.

Notice, though, that byzantine laws replace one kind of demand
of the ordinary person with another. Whereas the complaint about
the vague basic speed law is that ordinary people do not know what
counts as "safe and prudent," now they must keep track of five sections
and five subsections, and as a corollary keep track of the population
of towns they pass through, know when they are on an interstate or
other public highway, as well as the legal definition of daytime. This
is not a particularly tough challenge for an ordinary person for one

law, but multiply it by the number of traffic laws on the books and you have a clearly unreasonable expectation. Vague laws are supposed to have too little guidance value, but byzantine ones have too much of it.

BEHIND THE QUESTION OF whether vague laws or byzantine ones are better lies a very basic question; who do you trust? Edward Lawson and Rudy Stanko did not trust enforcers, and neither did the judiciary that ended up voiding those very laws for vagueness. On the other hand, legislative trust of law enforcement is what allows legislatures to formulate vague laws in the first place, delegating interpretive discretion to enforcers. When legislatures don't trust enforcers, you get mandatory enforcement policies.

Mistrust is the root of legalism. And the asymmetry between how easy it is to lose trust and how hard it is to restore it explains why we only seem to march toward legalism and never away from it. Mistrust is the common explanation for both laws of bureaudynamics. It takes one high-profile case of someone exploiting a loophole in a rule and getting away with it to transform entire institutions into legalistic ones. It takes generations of complex rule making, fanatical compliance officers, and overzealous bureaucracies gumming up efficient or effective governance for anyone to hint at the need for reform.

Mistrust, both its degree and its pervasiveness, drives the evolution of institutions toward less discretion and more complex rules that apply to rule followers, rule makers, and rule enforcers. Mistrust drives organizations toward legalism and away from their original goal, which was never compliance with an explicit set of detailed instructions but a spirit of cooperation for mutual benefit. And the unfortunate fact is that most of this mistrust is justified.

CHAPTER 5

MANDATES AND THE
NORMALIZATION OF LYING

————

RUSSELL CANAN ISN'T just a judge, he teaches judges. There's a judge school, the National Judicial College, where he teaches a course, Tough Cases. The course involves reading essays from a book of the same name that Canan coedited, about what it is like for judges to preside over morally and politically fraught cases, mostly high-profile cases of the 2000s such as Terry Schiavo, Elian Gonzalez, and Scooter Libby. It also addresses a host of lower-profile cases that have equally high stakes, like child-custody and eviction decisions. Canan wants his students to consider a question: when forced to choose, is a judge to follow law or follow justice?

RUSSELL CANAN WAS ONE of President Bill Clinton's first judicial appointments in 1993. About seven years into his term as superior court judge in Washington DC, Canan faced a tough case of his own. The case involved a middle-aged supermarket manager and part-time neighborhood DJ, Samuel Johnson. Johnson, a single father, took two of his young daughters, about thirteen and fifteen at the time, to a neighborhood party he was working. Two young men in their early twenties, Joe and William, started hitting on one of his underaged daughters. They complained about his music, insisting that he allow them to DJ. When Johnson relented, Joe blew out his speakers. Angered and exasperated, Johnson loaded his equipment into his car to leave. In the parking lot, Sam Johnson and William had a confrontation, and this is where the stories diverge.

Sam Johnson claimed William pulled out a gun, which Johnson then attempted to grab, and there was a struggle between the two. The gun went off, shooting William in the thigh. Frightened by this sudden turn of events and worried that William's friend Joe would emerge from the party to come after him, Johnson grabbed the gun, got into his car, and drove away, pulling over on the way home to throw the gun into a sewage drain.

William, on the other hand, claimed it was Sam who pulled out the gun. William claimed he turned to run away, and Sam shot him as he was fleeing. Why the wound was on the front of his thigh William could not explain, as everything happened so quickly. Maybe he turned back around before continuing to flee.

The gun was never recovered, and there was no record of Johnson ever legally owning a gun. Based on William's story, the prosecution brought Samuel Johnson up on three charges: assault with intent to kill while armed, assault with a deadly weapon, and possession of a firearm during a crime of violence.

These stacked charges against Johnson are a list of "lesser-included" offenses, meaning they are on a descending order of seriousness, but if Sam is guilty of the first, he's automatically guilty of the next two. The charges give room for a jury to find Sam guilty of the lesser offense and acquit him of the more serious ones. Of course, they could acquit him of every charge.

The important difference between each of these crimes is *mens rea*, or how evil or objectionable the perpetrator's state of mind is while committing the offense. Intending to kill someone with a weapon ranks highest. This state of mind is truly displaying the worst of human intentions. Second to that, mere assault with a deadly weapon is consistent with me just trying to hurt you, never intending to kill you with it. But by choosing a potentially lethal weapon to harm you, I place you at much higher risk of accidental death. This is a very bad state of mind, though not as bad as using a gun with the intent of killing you. The last charge references the least objectionable state of mind, as mere possession could mean that you had your gun properly holstered when you punched someone in the stomach, but it does not risk killing someone with the weapon.

A ranking of crimes by seriousness has in the last forty years become an important bureaucratic project. One way to think about criminal justice is that it is in the punishment business. And a basic tenet of the morality of punishment is that punishment should be proportionate to the severity of the crime. Having an official document ranking crimes by severity helps to ensure that sentencing judges do not violate this proportionality principle.

The years 1984 to 2005 loom large in the legislative attempt to remove discretion from the criminal justice system. In addition to being the year of introduction of mandatory-arrest policies for domestic violence, 1984 was the year Congress passed the Sentencing Reform Act, creating the United States Sentencing Commission, a federal branch in the judiciary of nominated bureaucrats tasked with creating and updating a ranking system for crimes and mapping each crime onto a prison sentence. The guidelines were made mandatory for federal judges to follow. Twenty-two US states then came up with their own sentencing guidelines. The political context was a conservative-liberal alliance aiming to make sentencing more uniform across crimes, across judges, and across jurisdictions. For the tough-on-crime advocates, no more would there be soft judges letting dangerous criminals back on the street. For supporters of social justice, no more would we see the kind of racial, ethnic, or social-class disparities across prison sentences that had been endemic in US history.

The sentencing guidelines were aiming for a rule-of-law ideal: same crime, same time. They did not remove discretion in sentencing completely. Crimes fell into categories of severity from one to forty-three. Within each level there are ranges of sentences, zero to six months in prison for level 1, thirty years to life for level 42, life imprisonment for level 43. And there are point systems for judges to calculate whether someone is on the higher or lower end of their range. You get more points the worse your criminal history, for instance. Judges could exercise discretion by choosing within the three to five years indicated in the guidelines. In that way discretion was limited but not eliminated.

THE PROSECUTION HAD ONLY one witness, William, and its entire case rested on his story. William was a weak witness. Judge Canan did not believe his story; it was incomplete and contradictory. He was arrogant and aggressive on the stand. He had a history of criminal activity, some very serious crimes, that came out in cross-examination when the defense was impeaching him. Judge Canan fully believed Sam Johnson's side of the story.

When the prosecution rested, the defense moved to have the case dismissed, or technically a *motion for judgment of acquittal,* requesting the judge to acquit the defendant before the case ever goes to the jury. The defense will make such a motion when they suspect a judge will think there is insufficient evidence to make the charge stick.

"Why didn't you just use your discretion and grant the motion at this stage?" I asked Judge Canan, knowing that he ruled against it.

"I had the power to do it, but I think that would have been a *lawless decision*," he responded.

A lawless decision, according to Canan, is when a judge makes a decision "contrary to law to reach a result that the judge wants to achieve." Canan wanted Samuel Johnson acquitted. But the law on motions for judgment of acquittal did not allow it. You don't throw a case out because you believe the defendant is not guilty. You don't even throw the case out if you think the evidence tells pretty decisively that the defendant is not guilty. You only throw a case out if you believe the prosecutor's evidence is so bad that no reasonable juror could possibly convict. And it wasn't *that* bad, Canan reasoned. Some juror could have believed William. Some juror could interpret Sam fleeing the scene as a sign of his guilt. They'd be wrong, in Judge Canan's eyes, but they would not be *unreasonable*. Such hypothetical jurors could vote to convict Sam. So while Judge Canan believed Sam's story, he could not, in keeping with the wording of the law, use his discretion to dismiss the case.

Which makes what happens next even more puzzling. The defense, it turned out, had a secret witness, an impartial eyewitness to the entire event, someone who happened to be out with a date strolling on the street. The witness did not live in the neighborhood, did not know the parties involved, and did not want to be involved, so he never came forward. The prosecution did not know about him. An investigator working for the defense team heard some neighborhood gossip that there was such a person, rumors they traced back to the date, who lived in the neighborhood. The investigator knocked on the witness's door and somehow convinced him to testify. They never informed the prosecution of this witness, most likely to cut off any possibility that the prosecution would find information that would undermine his credibility. It was a gamble. A prosecutor could just as easily have believed this witness and dismissed the charges against Sam.

The witness's testimony entirely corroborated Samuel Johnson's story. He, like Sam Johnson, was a good witness and thoroughly consistent on the stand. He came across as sympathetic and had no reason to lie. Judge Canan believed the witness. He thought the jury believed the witness. He suspected even the prosecution started to believe the witness. He told his law clerk at the conclusion of testimony that this would be a quick not-guilty verdict.

"You didn't feel even at that point that you had the authority to throw the case out?" I asked, returning to the motion for a judgment of acquittal. "Could you talk me through why that's true?"

"Well, for the same reason," he replied. "The judge is not the judge of the facts in a jury trial. The jury could either believe or not believe William or Sam and Sam's witness. That was their prerogative to either believe it or not. It is not the judge's prerogative to substitute the judge's viewpoint for the jury's."

The defense's evidence, according to the law concerning motions of acquittal, is almost entirely irrelevant. The wording is that a judge needs to assess the evidence "viewed in a light most favorable to the prosecution." It means that the judge must assume that everything the prosecution presents is true, and everything the defense presents is not, unless it corroborates the prosecution's evidence. Every contradiction must be resolved in favor of the prosecution. No matter how convincing the defense's case, if a motion for judgment of acquittal is made, Judge Canan is instructed to "unhear" it when it disagrees with the prosecution's evidence. So according to law, nothing had changed. In reality, though, a lot had changed.

What happened next was what made the case a tough one, where even Canan had to ask himself, *is it law or justice that we're seeking?*

The jury went to deliberate, and it was not a quick acquittal. Instead of reaching a verdict by the end of the workday, the jury adjourned at five and began deliberating again at nine thirty the next morning. At ten thirty, the jury returned with a question.

"Are we allowed to convict Samuel Johnson of assault with a deadly weapon without convicting him of assault with intent to kill?"

When Judge Canan saw the note, his stomach sank. He read it out loud for all to hear. It was an easy question to answer. He had already answered it, in writing, when giving instructions to the jury. Of course, the jury could convict the defendant of a lesser charge while acquitting him of the more serious charge.

Canan, the prosecution, and the defense were united in believing that the note was a sign that the jury was voting to convict Samuel Johnson of assault with a deadly weapon. There was no reason for the jury to be asking the question at this stage unless that was what they were planning to do. They were asking for permission to issue the conviction.

Here was the problem for the good judge. Assault with a deadly weapon entailed the charge of possession of a firearm. This latter charge carried a mandatory minimum of five years. Given that Sam was a single father, given that Sam was innocent of the charge, Canan believed this outcome was a serious miscarriage of justice.

"I didn't think sentencing Sam to prison for five years was justice. Especially for something I didn't think he did," Canan tells me.

After Canan read the note out loud in court, he told the parties what he thought of the case. He did not believe Sam deserved five years in prison, and he had no intention of sentencing Sam to five years. So he instructed the parties to get together, work out a plea deal that would make it so that Sam did not have to face five or even any years in prison.

It wasn't just a gamble; it was a flouting of his power. But to get to justice, Canan thought it was necessary.

"And much to my surprise," continued Canan, "the prosecutor, who was a very fair-minded person, came up with a deal."

Sam was to plead guilty to the more serious charge, assault with intent to kill with a firearm. This was a felony carrying a minimum of fifteen years in prison, according to federal guidelines, but that minimum was not mandatory. Judge Canan had discretion in sentencing for this crime. Since he already made clear in court that he was not going to send Sam to prison, it was to Sam's advantage to take this plea. In return, the prosecution would drop the other lesser-included charges.

Sam Johnson, for his part, did not want to take the deal. He had just testified, under oath, that he had not assaulted someone with the intent to kill them. Now he had to admit that he did do such a thing, again under oath, and have it on his record, be a permanently convicted felon, all to avoid prison time he didn't deserve in the first place. Sam started crying inconsolably, as did his daughters. He did not want to take the deal and didn't think that he could compose himself enough to do it in open court.

"All of a sudden, I hear this on the door," says Canan, as he knocks on his desk, "from behind the judge's bench, which led to the jury room. They had a verdict."

Sam had to decide before Canan brought out the jury. Canan did not think he could hold off the jury indefinitely, so he gave everyone fifteen minutes, after which he needed to get the jury home, verdict or not.

FROM 1986 RIGHT UP through 2018, the mandatory minimum was a favorite tool of lawmakers to show the public just how tough they were on particular crimes of public concern. In reaction to the moral panic around drugs plaguing urban areas in the 1980s, there were mandatory minimums of ten years for possession of sufficient amounts of heroin or cocaine and twenty years if dealing such drugs resulted in bodily injury or death. In reaction to a moral panic concerning pedophilia in the late 1980s, there was a federal mandatory minimum of twenty-five years for possession of child pornography. In reaction to gruesome murders by repeat offenders, there were mandatory life sentences in California for the "third strike," or third felony, conviction. And in reaction to an increase in gun-related crimes in the metropolitan DC area, there was a five-year mandatory minimum for possession of a firearm during the commission of a violent crime. Unlike the ranges that are part of the guidelines, mandatory minimums remove judicial discretion altogether. They are sentence mandates issued from lawmakers.

WITHIN FIFTEEN MINUTES, Samuel Johnson composed himself well enough to report that he was accepting the plea deal. But to do so, there needed to be a formal question-and-answer period between him and the judge. These were usually more ritualistic than substantive, but the Kafkaesque circumstances were not lost on Judge Canan, as the questions themselves took on a particular air of absurdity.

"Mr. Johnson, you are taking this plea under oath and what that means is if you lie under oath you could be charged with the crime of perjury or making a false statement. Do you understand?" Judge Canan asked.

"Yes, your honor," Sam replied.

"Has anyone forced, threatened, or coerced you to plead guilty?" Canan asked.

Sam looked right at him, for just a moment longer than made Canan comfortable.

"No, your honor," he replied.

"Has anyone promised you what sentence you are going to receive?"

Sam continued to look at Canan.

"No, your honor."

"WHAT WAS GOING THROUGH your mind at the time?" I asked Judge Canan in 2023, more than twenty years later.

"I had implicitly promised him he wasn't going to prison," Canan replied. "And I realized I shouldn't do that. Then I paused and I thought, Sam's lawyer wants him to do this. Sam wants to do it. The prosecutor wants him to plead guilty. How could this not be justice?

If all the key players in the system want a particular outcome, how could that not be justice?"

And furthermore, if this was justice, it was justice without an *improper* use of discretion. Canan did not feel he was in a position to dismiss the case even now, with the motion for acquittal right there and an excuse to grant it. That decision would not be reversible, would not be reviewable by an appeals court, and would acquit Sam Johnson for good, rather than saddle him with a serious felony record. But that decision ran afoul of the explicit standards in the law, whereas there was no law against a judge giving his opinion to counsel that a certain outcome was unjust and persuading the parties to work out a plea bargain so he did not have to issue such an outcome.

And so just like that, Judge Canan accepted the guilty plea, under oath, in the US Superior Court, where everyone who was present, even the prosecutor, knew that Samuel Johnson did not assault someone with the intent to kill. At that point Canan ordered Samuel Johnson released until sentencing and adjourned the court.

WHEN JUDGES ISSUE SENTENCES they deem most appropriate from a range of legally acceptable sentences, they are practicing *adjudicative* discretion. Adjudicative discretion is given to enforcers who issue *verdicts*, usually against a backdrop of considerations they are supposed to apply. These considerations leave open, at the end of deliberation, what the exact verdict is supposed to be. Other bureaucrats who practice adjudicative discretion include border patrol or immigration service agents when they decide who to let into a country, temporarily or indefinitely. In a nongovernmental context, some loan officers practice adjudicative discretion in deciding who gets a loan and on what terms. School or college admissions are yet another example.

Consider the following three factors that immigration officials are supposed to consider when deciding if someone should be admitted into the US.

Property or business ties in the United States;

History of taxes paid;

Evidence regarding respect for law and order, good character, and intent to hold family responsibilities (for example, affidavits from family, friends, and responsible community representatives).

The guidelines do not say how to take these factors into consideration. If an applicant has an uncle who owns an apartment complex in Queens, how heavily does that weigh? What if one of the affidavits from a sibling is just lukewarm? What if the applicant has a conspicuous lack of documentation for one of these factors? How much a consideration affects the final determination is entirely discretionary. The language in rule books sets the guidelines, and it might set a minimum threshold for qualification. But beyond that, verdicts are entirely discretionary.

HERE IS AN EXERCISE in adjudicative discretion. Suppose you are a small-business loan officer who needs to make a decision about Mr. X. Mr. X used to be a marketing consultant and has an invention for permanently reusable dental floss made out of self-sanitizing, indestructible carbon fiber. But each piece of dental floss currently costs $500, and Mr. X needs the loan to scale up production so as to reduce that cost to $300. Mr. X passes the minimal threshold for qualification: he has a good enough credit score, has been in business for a year, and has a $50,000 revenue stream. Mr. X is looking to borrow $200,000, and you have to make a judgment about the balance of "potential for success and risks of failure associated with a business of this kind" as well as "any employment history that is relevant to the success of the business." How are you supposed to weigh the potential success and risk of failure here? Do you think people would pay $300 for a single piece of forever dental floss?

It is easy to see that given ten different people, you will get ten different answers. Change any of these factors slightly and you may get different degrees of movement between different judges. What if Mr. X used to be a dentist? Some people might think that increases the chance of success, and some might think it lowers it. Either response is okay if you have adjudicative discretion.

For one kind of adjudicative discretion, everyone is weighing the same set of reasons, but they are allowed to weigh them differently, even significantly differently. If a judge puts zero weight on some factor, that amounts to ignoring it. This kind of adjudicative discretion has, built into it, the potential for a wide range of disparities in verdicts. In the criminal justice context, from the 1930s until the early 1980s, the US practiced indeterminate sentencing. Every person who committed a crime and was sent to prison received indeterminate time. Judges, parole boards, and prison officials determined whether the individual was ready to be released on a case-by-case basis. Many people, including prominent judges and policymakers, saw this system as greatly flawed, a sign that criminal sentencing was wild and lawless and in need of regulation and standardization. But there was method in this madness. Legal theorist Michael Tonry writes that this was an era where the aim of sentencing was reforming people. And most judges rightly observed that people differ. Some can be reformed; others cannot. Some can be reformed with a year's worth of jail time, others needed five or ten. So judges and parole boards took it upon themselves to determine how long any given individual ought to be imprisoned, revisiting cases regularly over time. Zoom out from that viewpoint to a large country with a large population, and it will look like thousands of people making very different decisions about the same Mr. X.

Another contribution to the wide disparity in verdicts resulting from adjudicative discretion comes from the fact that many jobs permit bureaucrats to expand the list of reasons they can use to issue their verdicts. US immigration, as well as criminal sentencing, has an "any other relevant factor" clause. If judges find any other factor that is relevant brought to their attention, they are allowed to consider it and weigh it as heavily as they want.

In one famous case in the Eastern District of New York, Judge Frederic Block decided in 2016 that he would factor something that no previous judges ever factored in determining a sentence. Many people who get convicted of felonies are no longer able to study for, apply to, or fill jobs such as teaching, nursing, barbering, general contracting, or dentistry. Others are disqualified from housing vouchers and student loans. Still others are prevented from living near schools or parks. Some face deportation; others will have their children taken away from them. These are long-term *collateral consequences* that an offender faces out in the world after a conviction, and for Judge Block, these kinds of government-imposed restrictions count as a kind of punishment for a conviction. Judge

Block reasoned that proportionality required him to subtract some comparable amount of punishment from a prison term if the government was going to impose additional punishment. No rule told Block to do this, and no rule prevented him from doing it. Instead, the rules left open a factor that others had ignored. It is unclear how many other judges weigh these kinds of reasons in issuing sentences. Adjudicative discretion allows all of them to do so.

There are two ways to narrow or eliminate adjudicative discretion altogether. One is to issue a blank mandate, a rule, blocking the available considerations or verdicts. For example, "nobody without family in the US will be allowed in" or "all people convicted of possessing child pornography receive twenty-five years" or "collateral consequences are not allowed as factors in sentencing." These mandates would have to come from legislatures. Mandatory sentences are examples of eliminating adjudicative discretion altogether.

Another way is to require algorithmic procedures for decision-making. You can have some bureaucracy design a form, flowchart, or piece of computer software that takes as input certain factors, preassigns all of the weights, and generates an output that is then decisive or close to decisive in determining the verdict. This manner of automating away discretion is rising significantly in the era of AI and big data. In the criminal justice context, individual offenders in many jurisdictions have an algorithm applied to various features of their lives—housing history, age, gender, criminal history—and assigned a *recidivism risk score*, exactly like a credit score. Judges see this score when they issue sentencing or other verdicts. No jurisdiction currently requires the score to be decisive; they are still only advisory. But they represent the wave of the future and will be discussed in the next chapter.

REMOVING ADJUDICATIVE DISCRETION WAS the ongoing pattern from 1984 through the next forty years. The Sentencing Reform Act, mandatory minimums, and mandatory postconviction collateral consequences together made the kind of thing that happened in Judge Canan's court a norm rather than an exception. This is the era of the *fictional plea*.

Legal scholar Thea Johnson defines a fictional plea as a plea to a crime, or facts of a crime, whereby every party to the plea, the defendant, prosecutor, and even the judge, knows that the crime or "facts" are fictions. Fictional pleas include examples like Samuel Johnson's, but they also include people who do commit crimes, but the harshness of the mandatory minimum and/or the collateral consequences prevent prosecutors and judges from imposing a particular charge. If the police report claims the defendant possessed a thousand grams of cocaine, the guilty plea will be to possession of ten grams, so that the defendant can keep custody of a child, for example. Part of a fictional plea deal might involve making up facts; for instance, to avoid being convicted of a single felony sex crime, an eighteen-year-old pleads guilty to three separate misdemeanor sex crimes, even though the defendant only committed a single crime. This kind of deal allows the defendant to avoid lifetime placement on the sex offender registry but also satisfies the prosecutor who wanted at least one year's imprisonment. Johnson mentions an example in Virginia of a defendant who pled guilty to firearm possession rather than marijuana possession, even though he was caught with marijuana and not a firearm, solely because the mandatory minimum in the case of firearm possession was more lenient.

Sometimes prosecutors make up crimes out of thin air. One

example, adapted from Johnson, would be pleading guilty to something like "attempted involuntary manslaughter." If you think about the meaning of these three words, such a crime is a contradiction in terms. A crime can't be both attempted (that is, intended) and involuntary. But according to Johnson, people have pled guilty to crimes like this to avoid any minimums or collateral consequences that might come with an involuntary manslaughter conviction.

When harsh and wide-ranging punishments become mandatory through legislation, the bureaucrats tasked with implementing criminal justice seek workarounds using their remaining discretionary powers. The result, the fictional plea, is something so common that when I ask judges, defense attorneys, and prosecutors about them, they simply call them "pleas." The fudging, ignoring, and rewriting of facts is so pervasive that it is a normal part of the system. Justice is no longer a matter of fact-finding and matching punishments with the moral wrongness and culpability of an offender. It is making up a fictional world in which the actual sentence of a person satisfies everyone. And people do end up satisfied with the process, as almost no one appeals a fictional plea to which they have agreed. So what can be wrong with it?

THE CASE OF SAMUEL JOHNSON did not end with the plea deal. After Canan accepted the plea, the jury returned in the Samuel Johnson case, ready to read their verdict. Judge Canan informed them that the defendant had pled guilty to the charge of assault with intent to kill and that he was grateful for the jury's service, but their verdict would not be necessary. Canan dismissed the jury and, surprised and confused, they got up to leave. Canan then returned to his chambers to prepare for another trial that began that afternoon.

The courtroom clerk went to the jury room to clean things up for the next trial and found a verdict note. The jury was going to acquit Samuel Johnson of all three counts.

"Legally that document meant nothing. I could have just tossed it in the trash can," Canan tells me, "but I thought it was only fair that the parties know about what happened." In fact, the jurors probably had already reported their verdict to prosecutors and defense counsel, as they were all speaking in the hallway. Canan called everyone back in and announced the content of the note.

"In the category of no good deed goes unpunished, I thought I had done the right thing for the right reasons, but it turned out, had I just done nothing, the right result would have happened," Canan reflects.

When asked if he would do it again, Canan is ambivalent. Under the circumstances with what was known at the time, it was a tough call. Doing nothing required a lot more faith than reason. But he now knew that the result of his intervention was worse than if he had done nothing.

In a few days, Sam's lawyer filed a motion to withdraw the guilty plea.

"The motion said that I," Canan reports, "the judge, had created a coercive atmosphere, and that but for my actions in suggesting the plea, he never would have done it. And therefore, that is grounds for withdrawing a guilty plea."

This bold but honest move essentially asked Canan to issue a verdict about his own misconduct. The prosecution protested, saying that if the verdict turned out the way everyone thought it was going to turn out, the last thing Sam would be doing was seeking to withdraw his guilty plea. So how can it be coercive if the verdict turned out one way, but not coercive if it turned out the other way?

"But I agreed with Sam's lawyer that there was a coercive atmosphere that was created. So I granted the motion to withdraw the guilty plea," says Canan.

At that point, the case officially ended in a mistrial. It was up to the prosecution to decide what to do with the case. They dismissed all charges.

I HAVE LONG THOUGHT about who the villain is in the story of Samuel Johnson. The legalist would say it is Russell Canan. He did not let the process play out the way it was supposed to. I used to think it was the prosecutor in the case, who brought a weak case against an innocent man on the testimony of an unreliable witness. This was a prosecutor who was still prepared to send Samuel Johnson to prison even after a reliable witness exonerated him. But in the end I could not place the blame on anything else but the mandatory minimum. Without the mandatory minimum, with full judicial discretion in sentencing, none of the turns in the story leading to the fictional plea would have been set in motion.

It is the lack of discretion under conditions of harsh penalties that is responsible for the Kafkaesque farces that pass for justice in the American criminal justice system. If it weren't for state-mandated harsh punishments, prosecutors, judges, and defense attorneys would not have to find all manner of strange, but legal, ways to bypass such penalties in situations where those penalties are morally abominable. There would be no need for institutionalized lying.

This kind of lying is not an exception in the justice system, it *is* the justice system in the era of fictional pleas. So what is wrong with a little fudging of fact, a little making up of crimes, if all parties agree to it and it gets the right result? Why is it a bad thing in the administration of justice?

The courtroom is supposed to be an institution of enforced truth telling. People swear oaths to the truth. Those oaths carry penalties of serious punishment. Whether your statements are true or false, you can expect them to be challenged. Generally speaking, truths are far easier to defend than falsehoods, because evidence for truths is more easily available than evidence for falsehoods. Court reporters document the official record of proceedings. Court transcripts are archived as the official record of what happened; historians hundreds of years from now will rely on them to give a factual account of history.

Of course, people lie in court, whether witnesses, defendants, or lawyers. But it does not mean that in the context of a courtroom lying is the aim. If lying is the aim of a courtroom, no one would be obligated to defend their claims when challenged, and listeners would not have a standing presumption to believe that speakers intend their claims to be believed. But we do have these presumptions, because we believe that everyone in a courtroom is held to the truth.

The era of fictional pleas is transforming the courtroom, and with it the official historical record of court proceedings. People are not really swearing to tell the truth, instead they are asked to say whatever is necessary to reach the right criminal justice outcome. Imagine if this transformation were explicit. Instead of "swearing to tell the truth, the whole truth, and nothing but the truth," individuals instead swear "to say whatever is necessary to reach the best outcome for myself." That is what Samuel Johnson was asked to do, under the pretense that he was swearing to tell the truth.

This is a deeply problematic move, especially for institutions of criminal justice. Situations where people are not held to the truth, but rather held to say whatever they have to say to get the right outcome, are dystopian ones. Partisan political rallies, especially fascist or cult rallies, are like this. Participants can say anything, true or false, as long as the statement serves the interest of the demagogue. Bald-faced lies, blatant untruths that everyone knows to be untruths, cannot be challenged in such a context, because everyone knows that the point is not to speak the truth. Blatant truths, no matter how commonly known, can be booed, challenged, and disregarded if they fail to serve demagogues' and their followers' interests in seizing political power. No evidence of truth or falsity is acceptable because the context is not one in which people care about truth or falsity.

The plea deal in the era of fictional pleas is turning criminal justice into an institution where the standard isn't truth—where the aim isn't fact-finding into what happened, how, and how do we know—but whether we can get a sentence right on a case-by-case basis. The empirical facts, sometimes even the legal facts, are merely instruments for that purpose. It is completely inappropriate for anyone present to challenge facts in a fictional plea; the aim is elsewhere. Justice in the era of sentencing mandates has been reduced to one goal, and it has reduced even good faith practitioners into agents of deception in the service of that goal.

OVER A SERIES OF decisions in 2004 and 2005, the US Supreme Court restored a great deal of adjudicative discretion to judges, overturning central features of the Sentencing Reform Act of 1984. In the *Blakely* decision (2004) and the *Booker* decision (2005), the closest possible majority of the Supreme Court ruled that mandatory federal sentencing guidelines were unconstitutional. Their reasoning is too complicated to go into for present purposes, but the result was that the guidelines became optional. Judges had to consider them but did not have to follow them. Mandatory minimums and collateral consequences, however, remain the law.

Still, the overturning of the Sentencing Reform Act makes for a natural experiment. In the federal courts before 1984, judges had a very wide range of adjudicative discretion. From 1984 to 2005, judges had the narrowest. Then, from 2005 until the present, there has been a mix, with Congress still passing mandatory minimums and appointed bureaucrats still setting out guidelines, but judges free to sentence outside of them. This history is a natural experiment: How do these periods compare?

A year after the *Booker* decision, the Bush Justice Department issued a memo arguing that the *Booker* decision had reintroduced everything that had been feared in 1984. Judges were once again accused of being too soft on criminals. The number of "downward departures" from the guidelines, shorthand for judges who sentenced people below the sentencing ranges, more than doubled, from 5.2 percent to 12.5 percent. The Bush Justice Department counted 8,100 downward departures from the guidelines in the year following *Booker*, and only 1,000 upward departures, or sentences higher than the guidelines. In addition, disparities increased. The report claimed that Black defendants received 4.9 percent higher sentences on average than white defendants and found that in the Northern District of Iowa "68.7 percent of defendants received sentences within the guideline ranges, while in the Southern District of Iowa, 48.0 percent of defendants received sentences within the guideline range." If race and geography do not affect the seriousness of crimes, why should there be such a disparity? The only answer, the DOJ argued, is that judicial discretion is perniciously biased in precisely the ways the Sentencing Reform Act of 1984 was trying to fix.

The trends that began during the Bush administration continued. Sentences became notably lighter after *Booker*, but disparities increased. By 2021, downward departures from the guidelines doubled, from 12.5 percent to 25 percent of cases. Meanwhile the average gap in sentences between two people who faced different judges for the same kind of crime more than doubled. It turns out, to no one's surprise, that whether judges are appointed by Democratic or Republican presidents or have tough or lenient dispositions toward defendants makes a difference to the length of sentence people get once you reintroduce judicial discretion.

There was also an increase in racial disparity after the *Booker* decision. According to the US Sentencing Commission's own models, the Black-white racial gap in sentencing increased by thirteen months largely due to judicial discretion. That is a very large increase. Independent scholars put the gap at more like two months.

A bigger driver of sentencing disparities post-*Booker* was how prosecutors reacted to the restoration of judicial discretion. Prosecutors increased their use of mandatory minimum charges for everyone, increased their *threats* of mandatory minimum charges, and increased their use of *binding pleas,* the kind of plea a judge cannot alter. They also did this disproportionately to Black defendants for drug crimes. It turns out that prosecutors might be more to blame for increasing racial disparities in sentencing post-*Booker* than judges, as prosecutors did a lot more to take sentencing out of the hands of judges than they did pre-*Booker*.

At the same time, defendants and their attorneys increasingly forewent clever pleas, fictional pleas, and creative pleas. Instead, more defendants pleaded honestly and truthfully to the crimes they committed in exchange for having robust sentencing hearings that allowed them to bring evidence before a sentencing judge about their personal histories and circumstances. It turns out that when judges have more discretion, defendants put more faith in judges and prosecutors put less.

People do not usually characterize the tough-on-crime era of American history as an era of mistrust of judges. But that is one way to understand the many mandates on sentencing, the proliferation of collateral consequences, and the increased power of the prosecutor and the plea deal. If judges cannot be trusted to implement a policy that punishes people the way legislators want them punished, the solution is to bypass them altogether. As evidenced in the post-*Booker* era, this mistrust is not entirely unfounded. Judges tend not to do what the masses or elected officials or even prosecutors want them to do.

So should we trust judges? This question cannot be answered until we determine what we want from judges if they have unfettered discretion. Should they answer to their internal sense of fairness, guidelines issued by legislators, mass democratic preferences and pressures, or, like doctors, best practices based on research by social scientists looking to measure interventions, harms, and rehabilitation? The question is not widely discussed or debated, even in jurisdictions where judges are elected. When we are not used to thinking about discretion, we do not think about how it ought to be exercised. So we do not know how to evaluate, reasonably and in a principled way, whether particular acts of judicial discretion are sound. Instead, we work from anecdotes and outrage, and codify them in law.

CHAPTER 6

THE COMING OF THE ROBOT RULERS

———

A RBITRARINESS THAT LEADS to injustice (as feared by Western liberals) and mediocrity that degrades society (as feared by Han Fei) together present a powerful case for legalism. Yet people who study bureaucracies do not usually fear the elimination of discretion, for even in the most legalistic of organizations, like professional sports or the Food and Drug Administration, discretion is impossible to eliminate. Human rule making and its enforcement is always imperfect, and discretion is a side effect of that imperfection. Such imperfections include:

(1) Economic limitations: no matter the rule, there is not enough money to hire enough enforcers and paperwork processors so that every violation of that rule will be caught and punished properly.

How many traffic cops and desk bureaucrats would we need to make sure every traffic violation is logged, the right person is charged with the right fine, and each fine is collected? Whatever the answer, there just aren't enough tax dollars to go around, and police departments will need to decide whether to prioritize dangerous intersections, or high traffic ones, or those fines most likely to be paid. Bureaucracy is a consequence of societies of scale; and when enforcement cannot keep up with the scale of rule breaking, you will need enforcers to use their judgment to prioritize.

(2) Technological limitations: we do not have the technical means to monitor every possible way and situation in which laws and rules can be broken.

Ordinary citizens, highly cognizant of bureaucracy, underestimate the sheer scale of rules and laws that would require surveillance for enforcement. There is, in fact, a law requiring the holes in every slice of Swiss cheese to be between three-eighths and three-quarters of an inch, with no more than a certain number of holes per slice. Given all the rules that exist and the lack of technology to detect all violations, we require human judgment to determine whether it is worth inventing universal Swiss-cheese-hole-detection devices.

(3) Linguistic limitations: laws, rules, procedures, and policies must be written with language, and language is inherently vague and open to interpretation.

This limitation seems to be decisive in leaving some kind of discretion even in the most legalistic of systems. Even in sports, where rule of law is a supreme value and characterizing impermissible physical contact between people of utmost importance, rules must employ vague language.

The final need for discretion in a legalistic organization comes from a human failure.

(4) Lawmaker lack of foresight: no one is smart enough to know in advance the perfect rules.

Yet these are practical, not moral, constraints on legalism. If there were some practical way to overcome these limitations, the legalist believes we should use it. We have to live with discretion as a necessary evil only because we cannot perfect the process of rule making.

Today, however, we can envision a society in which the evil of discretion is no longer necessary. Before the invention and cheap availability of surveillance cameras, we figured it was impossible to enforce every traffic law. But it isn't. California's automated red-light traffic enforcement, where sensors and cameras capture the running of red lights and send citations to registered owners of vehicles, has been used for a decade now. Tracking technology in electric cars may cover the rest within my lifetime. Electric cars can know not only a driver's speed, but their distance from other vehicles and pedestrians on the road. Cars can even track where a driver's eyes are looking and whether their hands are on the steering wheel. You can just as easily measure cabin sound levels and a driver's blood alcohol level. Reckless driving no longer needs to be a judgment call based on whether a cop has observed a particular vehicle from the outside. We can, if we want, issue tickets based on electronic car data and automatically dock fines from people's paychecks or bank accounts.

White-collar crimes are even easier to enforce. No economic or technological barrier prevents us from keeping a central database of all financial transactions and runing them through learning models that are incredibly good at forensic accounting, flagging irregularities that could signal financial crimes.

STANDARDIZED CREDIT SCORING WAS one of the earliest examples whereby a single algorithmically produced number assigned to every individual was able to remove judgment altogether from bureaucrats. Prior to the modern-day credit score, individual credit officers took lists of factors about a person's life to make a holistic human judgment about the likelihood they would pay back borrowed money. The credit score, which essentially plugs a list of factors about your financial history, like types of debt, payment history, and so forth, into a secret mathematical formula to generate a number, removed the need for adjudicative discretion in many financial matters. Institutions and to a large extent the general public simply accepted the use of credit scores, ignoring many of their flaws, spawning many similar tools meant to overcome the threat of arbitrariness and the disparities of human decision-making.

China's social credit system is a straightforward generalization from credit scores. Evidence about you is plentiful and trackable from your phone, subway cards, citations, lawsuits, and criminal history. All that evidence can be compiled and weighted to determine whether you qualify for public services, whether you should be admitted into a university, even which dates you qualify for on a dating site.

Lest the Western reader believe that this is a particularly gruesome idea from central planners of a totalitarian government, plenty of us have gladly decided to structure our diets and exercise routines, read books, watch movies, and go to restaurants according to centralized online scoring systems like Yelp, Google reviews,

Goodreads, Rotten Tomatoes, and lifestyle tracking apps that generate scores of their own. And many gig workers define themselves in their work through their Uber, Airbnb, or DoorDash ratings. Gig workers have no meaningful identity to their customer or employer. They are simply a job description and a number, representing the quality of their work. We do not meaningfully hire another *person* to drive us, house us, or feed us, we hire whoever inhabits a job with a higher than 4.5 rating. When we hire gig workers, we don't care about getting particular people, because people are completely interchangeable on gig apps. Han Fei would be delighted.

Criminal justice is beginning to use smart automation, too. Algorithmic risk assessment is now a standard tool in sentencing. Standardized sets of information about a defendant's age, gender, income, criminal history, housing history, employment history, and so forth get scored according to predetermined weights to generate a recidivism risk score, which is then passed on to a judge. Algorithmic risk assessment today is not particularly smart. The current set of tools is no more predictive of a person's risk of recidivism than ordinary discretionary judgment. But this, again, is a technological and practical, not a moral, complaint. If the tools get better, legalism implies that we have very good reasons to defer to them.

SOMETIME IN THE EARLY 2000s, the Educational Testing Service decided to design automated essay grading for their standardized tests. ETS is a company known for designing and implementing some of the most well-known standardized tests in the world, including the PRAXIS, TOEFL, GRE, and TOEIC exams. These exams determine major life plans for millions of people around the world. TOEFL scores help determine whether a student can get into a school of their choice in a country of their choice. TOEIC scores help international English learners tap the English-speaking job market. Writing ability is essential to doing well on these exams, and scoring essays used to be adjudicative discretion par excellence. People with college educations, trained by ETS on a set of samples, sat and read hundreds of essays a day and scored them based on a set of criteria.

It used to be that each essay had two human readers who scored them on a scale of one to five. The final score would be the average of the two, unless they were very far apart, in which case the essay went to a third reader, who would effectively issue a final score.

Then ETS started working on early natural language processing software that would read and score essays automatically. The software E-rater was programmed to generate a score based on features of an essay that ETS researchers took to correlate with good and bad writing, like word choice, word length, sentence length, sentence structure, and so forth. As early as 2004, almost twenty years before modern AI deep learning, E-rater was able to be more *consistent* than two arbitrary human readers. Humans will eventually disagree widely on a particular example. Take even one human out of the equation and the disparity reduces. Also, the need to pay that human judge disappears. Take all humans out of judging essays, and you will get a completely uniform scoring system and remove a lot of people from the payroll. It seems like a win-win. Removing adjudicative discretion is an explicit goal of decision automation.

Twenty years later, we have deep learning, which does not even need a human to tell it what to look for in an essay to score it. Instead, programmers tell the machine to read millions and millions of previous essays, and it tells the machine what score each of them got from the human readers. The machine will extract from this data a rule that generates the right score for every essay it has read. The rule will then be perfected by testing it on essays it has not read, by comparing the machine's score to the reader's score. This perfected rule will then be ready for open use, scoring new essays consistent with how human raters scored the millions of essays the machine has seen. Once the model has learned, it is going to outperform every mediocre scorer *by design*. No individual person can match their scoring ability to a machine that has trained to score identically to thousands of scorers over millions of essays.

A central feature of this kind of AI automation is that deep learning, and even the early ETS software, identifies *mathematical* rather than linguistic rules to reach verdicts. Human scorers are trained to give verdicts based on vague standards. Does an essay "convey ideas fluently and precisely using effective vocabulary and sentence variety?" Does an essay "demonstrate superior facility with the conventions of standard written English?" Does it display curiosity, open-mindedness, and insight? These criteria are what make essays good when humans judge them. There is simply no other way to teach a person how to score an essay than by telling them the criteria of a good essay. By contrast, the machine is counting the number of letters in words, the number of words in sentences, the number of times words are repeated, adding, multiplying, and dividing these numbers and others according to equations to calculate the very score hundreds and thousands of previous human readers would have given that essay if they were able to put their heads together and average out all of their flaws. Any program designed to do this, and do it well, will outperform any mediocre person. And it does so without any reference to vague linguistic rules.

With deep learning, the judgment of machines is getting very close to the judgment of people. Train a new human reader for a month and they might match trained, experienced readers 80 percent of the time. Use deep learning and the machine will match the best-trained human reader 95 percent of the time. When it doesn't, it is the humans who have to second-guess themselves.

In another sense, however, machine judgments are getting farther apart from—and almost alien to—human judgment. Earlier technologies like ETS's E-rater follow precise mathematical instructions, rather than vague linguistic ones, but its mathematical rules are at least explicable in human terms, because its rules were formulated by humans. Engineers could tell you, "This equation is calculating word lengths and word repetitions and rewarding essays that use longer words that are not repeated much." By the time deep learning generates accurate verdicts for new essays, circa 2024, no language can even in principle describe what the equations are doing, what with their hundred billion terms and arithmetical operations. These are equations for which there is no explanation in human language. A programmer can show you this equation, though you could never read it for its length, and the only coherent description of what it means is "this is the equation that fits all the past verdicts the best." Deep learning is not just opaque, it is humanly indecipherable. Deep-learning rules are the logical endpoint of the proliferation of rules. It is the endpoint of legalism, where the laws of bureaudynamics take us in the most extreme case, where no one even understands the rules that govern us.

SCORING ESSAYS AND GIVING criminal justice verdicts are alike enough that deep learning is the future of adjudicative discretion.

A lot of the information given to judges and juries today is already the output of deep-learning systems like facial or license plate recognition, algorithmic risk assessment scores, accounting forensics, and crime scene reconstruction. Data about millions of arrestees are already in wide use for deep-learning models. It is not a question of if, but when, the millions of criminal cases we have texts of, and the millions of verdicts already on the record, get placed into deep-learning programs so we have a tool for generating verdicts in future cases. Then disparity and arbitrariness will disappear.

This is one possible path for the future of justice, a kind of techno-optimism. I would hazard to predict that without explicit policy decisions to the contrary, this is the foreseeable path of institutions of scale generally and criminal justice in particular.

How deep does our mistrust of humans run? Does it run deeper than our mistrust of machines? If you find the legalist, techno-optimist vision a utopia, you long to live in the society envisioned by Han Fei. If you find it repulsive, you will need to locate what went wrong in our reasoning as we took the march to legalism.

CHAPTER 7

FROM FEWER RULES
TO BETTER PEOPLE

———

I WAS TRAVELING THE country giving talks one fall, and my host at a prominent institution decided to organize a morning roundtable discussion that began at 9:30 am. Naturally she wanted to order coffee. Apparently they have a rule about coffee purchases. All catering must be done through a specific vendor, a vendor that does not operate until after ten. There is a Starbucks two buildings over from the event that opened at seven thirty, which was fully capable of filling the order. The administrator in charge would not authorize the purchase because Starbucks was not the approved vendor. But the approved vendor subcontracts its coffee services to Starbucks. The receipts almost always indicate the purchase of Starbucks coffee, mostly likely from the very same branch the administrator was refusing to preapprove. Surely, my host argued, this was enough evidence that this coffee purchase was within the spirit of the rules. The administrator disagreed and did not approve the purchase. It was against the rules.

Western liberal political philosophers envision tyrants and their penchant for arbitrariness as a great threat to civilization. They are right. Tyranny has done as much as anything else to keep humans from flourishing. Western liberals have been less concerned with a figure who is the opposite of the tyrant in disposition but no less to be feared. This is the by-the-book bureaucrat. These bureaucrats are naturally inclined toward legalism and deeply afraid of exercising discretionary judgment. They do not want the responsibility; they fear all blowback so they are highly risk averse. Confronted with a decision they are unsure about, they look up the governance language and are comforted when they find that the issue is out of their hands. If someone goes to the by-the-book bureaucrat with a novel idea, the only way to get them to yes is if there are explicit rules in favor of the idea. Otherwise the bureaucrat will not want to set a precedent or risk any flak, even if they have the power to say yes.

By-the-book bureaucrats are the modern-day archetype of the Han Fei ideal; they envision themselves not as people engaging with other people, but as inhabiting a role, the role of the rule follower. They love job titles and job descriptions for themselves and those they manage, because titles and descriptions take decisions out of their hands. By-the-book bureaucrats do not simply need to stay within the rules, they need to stay *safely* within the rules.

Of the many objectionable qualities of surveillance-state legalism, the most serious is how bad it is for the moral and social character of the people who live in and run such societies. True, there are the familiar and uncontroversial critiques of surveillance states. We cannot trust governments in all of their mediocrity to do bad things only to bad people while leaving the rest of us alone. Eventually governments will do bad things to all people, harassing minorities, muckrakers, and political dissidents. But I think that even worse than this is the effect such societies have on the obedient. The goal of surveillance-state legalism is to turn all citizens into compliance robots and every bureaucrat into a by-the-book bureaucrat. It does this by turning human motivation in all of its rich complexity into fear of stepping out of line and into a love of acting for the sake of rules. This is the true horror of legalism.

Let us define a person who acts *solely for the sake of legal reasons* as a person who is motivated only by legal rules and penalties. Acting for the sake of legal reasons, unlike tyranny, is not always to be eschewed. A corporation, for example, might refrain from dumping toxic waste into the Hudson River, not because its board thinks it is immoral but because of legal constraints. In that case I am just glad the toxic waste isn't in the river. It doesn't much matter to me why. But does this generalize to all matters?

When my daughter was eight, we acquired two pet bunnies on the condition that she was responsible for them. As with her dish-washing chore, things started out fine. She even looked up extensive caretaking videos and went about critiquing other people's failures at rabbit care. But over time the quality of care declined. She left their water bowls dirtier than I liked. The rabbits occasionally had insufficient amounts of hay, and she did not brush them nearly enough. We made a checklist of best practices and evaluated her work twice a day. But after a while, the caretaking lapsed. Three years later, things still ebb and flow, and compliance is not 100 percent. What is true of her dishwasher chore became true of her bunny chore. We explored some rewards and penalties. That lasted a few weeks, but there were periods where she simply accepted the penalty and allowed the chore to lapse. We could have escalated the penalties and rewards. But we have not.

In fact, I even took the dishwasher rule off the refrigerator. It is not that compliance has gotten better or stern warnings have disappeared. I occasionally do some checking and admonish her when things look egregious. But I concluded that if you run your household like a legalist, whether it is with families or roommates, if you have to start piling paragraph-long rules into books and issue rewards and penalties like a Qin-era administrative accountant just to get someone to wash the dishes and feed their rabbits, you're doing something wrong. As a parent, as a person, you done messed up.

When it comes to doing chores in the home, I do not want mere compliance in my child, I want consideration. The aim of creating responsibilities and holding her to them is not for her to act for the sake of the rules and the punishment and rewards they bring. We want her to feed, water, and brush her bunnies because they are vulnerable living things whose well-being depends completely on their caretakers. We want her to empty the dishwasher in a timely way because it is important for a kitchen to be clean and useful, because it is essential not to be a free rider in the home, and because you have obligations to other people. We want to cultivate in her the spirit and reasoning behind the rules, especially when they are good ones.

We also want her to have the judgment to figure out when rules are not good, either because the rationale behind them is flawed or because she has figured out a better way to do things. Maybe she disagrees that keeping the rabbit hay box full at all times is the best practice. Maybe she finds that our bunnies need more exercise and are more active when they have less food. The development of this kind of judgment, as well as the motivation to execute that judgment, is far more important than following rules set down by others.

It isn't that I think legalism doesn't work. Make the penalties severe and consistent enough and I'm sure I could get better, more consistent compliance. But if my child ends up being the administrator who refuses to approve the coffee purchase, I have failed to raise a decent, reasonable person as much as I would have failed if I raised a tyrant. Choose between a world of apparatchiks who follow the letter of the law and a world of imperfect decision-makers who have judgment and motivation to do well by the spirit of the rules, who are ready to identify better ways to do things, I'll take the latter 100 percent of the time.

Even in sports, where I consider a rule of law ideal, we do not like players who act solely for the sake of legal reasons. An NBA player should refrain from clotheslining an opponent, not because the foul rules now explicitly prohibit clotheslining, but because he should be thinking about his moral obligations to his fellow players. If it is fair game to injure an opponent for the sake of winning, he should reconsider his purpose. He should also be thinking seriously about the corruption of his own soul, as the ancient Greeks would put it, if he needs a rule book to figure out whether to strangle another person when playing basketball.

Acting solely for the sake of legal reasons is a flaw, not a goal, of human beings. It is not morally praiseworthy nor desirable to live in a household or society or to work for a company where the sole reason for compliance is fear of punishment or self-interested benefit. People should drive at a safe speed to help protect the lives of others. Children should do their chores because parents need their help. Players should not engage in unsportsmanlike conduct because it makes them awful people and awful players.

If I must run my household like a legalist to get compliance, then I have not cultivated an environment in which the real reasons—why the rules are there in the first place—are appreciated and serve as motivations for my housemates. The moral worth of someone complying with rules does not come from the compliance, it comes from the underlying motivations and reasons someone has for such compliance.

In addition, there may be plenty of moral worth in not complying with rules, as I hope this book has illustrated. As many people have long pointed out in the study of discretion, rules are bound to reach their limits as times change and unforeseen circumstances arise. Making a lewd gesture at an opposing player is unsportsmanlike and can very well run afoul of the spirit of the rules of a game. But gestures count as lewd depending on cultural norms. There may be no explicit prohibition against a gesture that suddenly in 2024 becomes racist or sexually explicit. Will a referee call it? What if the rules explicitly prohibit a gesture that was lewd in 1891 but now means nothing? Does the referee call this one? It depends on whether these referees have good judgment. Novel circumstances will require judgments based on the reasons behind the rules. People who live out of fear of noncompliance will have no idea what to do in such circumstances. Even worse, they will apply rules in ways contrary to the reasons those rules exist in the first place. They will act unjustly under the cover of law, whether it is in denying coffee or denying freedom.

But more important, even if the rules cover all the cases we want them to cover, even if legislative bureaucrats find the right byzantine rule with every exception formulated precisely, we have good reasons not to be legalists. The moral quality of an individual and the standards of excellence in athletics, firms, and organizations rest on the quality of reasons motivating people's actions. There is something highly objectionable about behavior solely or even primarily guided by legal reasoning. People who care for their children because it would be illegal to neglect them are not particularly good people.

So being answerable to laws and rules is not a good enough guide for being a high-quality human being. When we tell children that the reason to do something is because those are the rules and breaking them is punishable by force, we are being bad parents. These are explanations of desperation, not wisdom. It is a terrible message. The real reason why children should be doing something, if they indeed should be doing it, is because it is the right and proper thing for people to be doing in that circumstance, because of morality, because of self-respect, because it is best for their future selves. The mere fact that it also happens to be a rule that comes with punishment is secondary. We need to articulate the genuine reasons behind rules and have people develop the judgment to assess those reasons and be motivated by them.

What is true for people who are the subjects of rules is also true for enforcers. Referees and umpires, police, prosecutors, and judges, all street-level bureaucrats who act solely on the basis of legal reasons, are not people who cultivate the right reasons for actions, reasons that can motivate the right action in novel circumstances. There is a reason we think of Officer Mike as not only acting well by Joey but doing *good policing*. There is a reason that Judge Canan, who was acting contrary to the letter of law regarding the mandatory minimum, was still acting in the spirit of the law, which is to issue fair and proportionate punishment. There is a reason that Judge Frederic

Block, the federal court judge who decided to factor collateral consequences into his sentencing decisions, is a hero, not a legalist villain, when he noticed and counteracted the US government's double punishing of defendants. Good enforcers develop independence of moral judgment, so that not every judgment is beholden to laws and standardized procedures.

Enforcers who are by-the-book bureaucrats can serve no check on bad rules, bad law, or even good laws that are out-of-date or that have hit their limits. There was probably a rationale to the no-catering-purchases-except-through-this-vendor rule. Maybe there was a history of profligate spending on catering orders or up-charging by other vendors. But in the context of needing coffee for an event at 9:30 am, the rule needed an exception. There was a rationale for tough-on-crime drug laws during the rise of drug use in the 1980s. There was a possible world in which those laws worked and deterred drug crimes. In that world, shortly after passage, the fear of harsh punishment deterred almost all drug users and traffickers, the drug problem went away, and those laws seldom had to be enforced. That is the world that legalism predicted. But it did not happen. Mandates and penalties and strict enforcement never solved the problem. Instead, the laws decimated communities for generations.

Laws do not receive moral or practical legitimacy simply by virtue of being passed by a legislative body, not even a democratically elected one. There are plenty of bad laws and laws that used to be good but are now bad. What if a certain social problem remains even when you punish it by death, torture, war? What then? Legalism is completely silent when punishments and rewards stop working. If all enforcers are by-the-book bureaucrats, they will never exercise intelligence or independence of judgment to mitigate the harms of bad law.

There is a role for everyone to evaluate law—citizen, enforcer, and legislator alike—even if we think people should not be able to overturn law at their own whim. Bad laws followed blindly and enforced unquestioningly have just as much chance to destroy good governance as the mediocre leader making mediocre decisions. Discretionary acts are an organization's way to build in checks on the moral and practical legitimacy of laws and rules. We need wise enforcers when legalism hits its limits, and even when it doesn't. Wise enforcers, like wise citizens, make a society worth living in. They are part of the "good" when we say we want to live in a good society.

The figure of the by-the-book bureaucrat shows us something else that is fundamentally flawed about legalism: it is self-defeating. When the legalist takes us on a path to increasingly precise and detailed rules, culminating in mathematical formulas, arbitrariness returns with a vengeance, the very thing legalism was supposed to be fighting. I recently witnessed a store clerk request a photo ID from someone clearly over fifty attempting to buy nonalcoholic beer and then deny the purchase because the ID was expired. There was nothing he could do, he claimed, because of the way the computer system was set up. The bureaucrat who refused to approve the coffee order was not acting for good reasons. The reason was, in fact, utterly stupid. Rules implemented in a techno-surveillance state, whether by AI or a by-the-book bureaucrat, will round up every last rule breaker and treat each the same, making no distinctions where there is a genuine moral difference. This is the hallmark of arbitrary enforcement.

When you impose a precise rule on something as complex as human behavior, arbitrariness will follow. Consider the many precise

age requirements that pervade the law. Drinking laws in the US prohibit people under the age of twenty-one from purchasing alcohol.
There are consent laws, voting laws, gambling laws, even rules about
participation in full-contact karate. The rationale is familiar; there
is a level of maturity and growth required before people are responsible enough to be given independent access to certain things. That
level of maturity, though, varies by individual, and maybe by culture.
Some sixteen-year-olds are mature and responsible enough to drink,
some twenty-five-year-olds (or maybe even fifty-year-olds) are not.
The cutoff of twenty-one or eighteen or sixteen is arbitrary. Any cutoff will fail to distinguish between a mature sixteen-year-old and an
immature twenty-five-year-old. The right reason to restrict someone
from voting or drinking is because of their immaturity, not because
they fall on one side of a particular age line.

As it goes with age cutoffs, it also goes with other cutoffs. Blood
alcohol measurements are an imperfect tool for distinguishing
between drivers who are too intoxicated to drive safely and drivers who are not. Any DUI officer can give you examples of people
who blow twice the legal limit and can pass every coordination test.
Many of us know an alcohol lightweight. Half a glass of wine and
you wouldn't feel safe letting them operate a lawnmower. But the
law gives a cutoff of .08 percent, so anyone who blows over that limit
will be subject to a DUI arrest, no matter how safely they are able to
drive. This is not a critique of the law, it is an observation about how
it applies. The law has replaced the potential arbitrariness of human
judgment with the arbitrariness of a blind rule.

There is no better example of how precise rules engender arbitrariness than with AI. ETS's E-rater software grades essays on the
basis of a set of equations precisely separating out level-4 essays from

level-5 essays with no vagueness in its criteria. The equations make it mathematically possible for two nearly identical essays to be scored differently, with one receiving a 4 and the other a 5, simply because the first contained the phrase "long word" and the second had "sesquipedalian." This is because the algorithm is *sesquipedalophilic*: it includes a formula that rewards longer words, everything else being equal. Take it from someone who has graded essays for twenty years, no human grader would be impressed enough with "sesquipedalian" to move an essay from a 4 to a 5 on that basis alone. (Okay, maybe on a bad day.)

And unlike with human graders, the AI will consistently, predictably make this move. AI is like any by-the-book bureaucrat who, settling on the rule that prohibits coffee purchases from any vendor but A, will give you no explanation as to why vendor A can purchase Starbuck's coffee but you cannot. Asked why that rule is the right rule, they insist only that it is the rule.

The idea that AI is so smart that it can remove arbitrariness has things backward. AI is actually so dumb that it introduces arbitrariness by making distinctions where there are none. And it cannot make the right distinctions if a rule does not tell it to. AI follows its complex instructions and equations so precisely in novel cases that it thinks like, well, a robot. You can solve the problem of predictability and consistency with AI but not the problem of arbitrariness.

In the criminal justice context, this consequence of AI is downright frightening. Suppose an AI algorithm has determined (truthfully) that age is a big risk factor for recidivism. If an AI is asked to give a verdict between "indefinite detention" or "release pending trial," there will be examples where a twenty-nine-year-old who is one day shy of their thirtieth birthday gets sent to jail while a thirty-year-old gets released, all other things being equal, because the algorithm makes numerically precise cutoffs. That decision is no less arbitrary than one judge who sends the twenty-nine-year-old to jail and another judge releasing the thirty-year-old. AI is a by-the-book bureaucrat making arbitrary judgments with rules. The opponent of arbitrariness should be hostile to AI, not welcoming of it.

The lesson we should learn from AI is that, as bad as arbitrariness in human judgment can be, the alternative is worse. At the very least, human-generated arbitrariness is explicable. The reasons for it are easily understood: prejudice, fatigue, ignorance, greed, or cognitive decline. We understand these things because we are subject to them. On the other hand, machine-generated arbitrariness, when it is done in the deep-learning model, is inexplicable. There is no way for AI to answer for an arbitrary decision and no way to hold it accountable or to correct for a decision made arbitrarily. Neither it nor we can explain any verdict it gives, good or bad.

In addition, we know that current AI research programs simply encode human biases, provided those biases are systematic. AI is an aggregator of human discretion of the past. It will only be as good as the totality of all human judges of the past. If AI wins and replaces human discretionary judgment in the future, then it will have no data from humans in the future to learn from, and humans of the future will be unable to see how much they can improve on judgments of humans of the past. The result of deferring to AI at any point is that it makes all subsequent verdicts a slave to the arbitrary standards of past humans. And that we know to be a source of unfairness—only this kind of unfairness cannot be rectified by learning and growth.

In human affairs, no matter how we structure rules and discretion, some degree of arbitrariness will remain. We have learned to live with it, even accept it, in some facets of life. Many people have felt the apparent injustice of receiving a speeding ticket for going eighty in a sixty-five zone while a hundred other cars are going eighty, perhaps even faster. That really is a disparity of treatment, a disparity of enforcement. The rationale traffic cops give for this kind of enforcement is that they are unable to ticket everyone going eighty, so they pick one person at random and ticket them. It is within their right to do this, and it is also quite arbitrary. But many of us live with it and are not particularly bothered by it. This kind of arbitrariness is unfortunate, but it is not *unfair*.

What concerns us with justice and injustice is fairness, not arbitrariness and not disparity per se. There is nothing fairer for instance than using a lottery or random chance to select winners and losers. It might not be wise, but fair lotteries place everyone on a level playing field. Let's say a prestigious university is unable to distinguish between the academic and extracurricular records of two students, A and B. But they can only let in one. Any selection process is arbitrary, but flipping a coin is perfectly fair. What violates fairness for many people, leading to anger and lawsuits, is using some other criterion to break the tie, one that people find objectionable. For example, having a rich parent or a parent who is an alumnus, or being a famous actor, and most contentiously, being Asian or Black. Lotteries make selection insensitive to normative factors, and in that it makes selection arbitrary. But they also make selection insensitive to irrelevant factors, and in that there is fairness.

The legalist and techno-optimist are right that there is a great deal of unfairness that results from human discretion. Class, racial, gender, or religious biases are unfair. Other biases are unfair, like catching a judge or cop on a bad day. And many reasons for disparate enforcement are unfair, like corruption or using citizens as a piggy bank by issuing tickets or citations and seizing assets. These biases make it so that classes of people, with no moral difference from others, are not entering a fair lottery. This needs to be rectified. Reviewing and improving human decision-making is the way to do it, not legalism. Legalism overcorrects and tries to eliminate even chancy parts of human discretion in favor of rules that introduce arbitrariness in other ways. It is a fact of human interactions that there will be some randomness in decision-making. This is a source of arbitrariness, but not injustice. The techno-optimist simply assumes that the arbitrariness of AI rules is better than human randomness. This assumption is false.

THIS BOOK HAS BEEN a long argument, empirical and philosophical, for the value of discretionary decision-making in criminal justice and in organizations of scale more generally. But there are legitimate reasons for legalism, that is, for turning to increasingly complex rules and mandates for their enforcement. The rule of law is a real value and a check against despotism. Bias in human decision-making is a well-known reality that is hard to correct. Mediocrity is a very serious threat to scaling up anything, whether a state agency, a sport, or a restaurant franchise. There is virtue in the predictability of standardization and of living in large-scale societies and organizations.

So how do we increase discretion in a system whose logic is to march toward legalism, in a system of mediocre and possibly unjust enforcers and inevitably rule breakers? I am a philosopher, not a policymaker or reformer, so I can give only the most abstract and tentative of ideas. Here is my proposal:

(1) Build discretion into all top-down mandates, essentially allowing for exceptions.

This has been the overarching theme of the criminal justice portions of this book. We should allow street-level bureaucrats to make exceptions in the cases where morality requires that they be made, in the cases where shoplifting isn't a jailable offense or where a particular drug possessor does not deserve ten years in prison or where purchasing Starbucks coffee is not a corrupt act. No matter that a rule maker can't envision an exception, it will arise, so give selective discretion to your enforcers.

(2) Live with interpretive discretion.

In my own life, I have come to embrace the virtues of vague rules, knowing full well their pitfalls, that is, bad calls made by mediocre people. I do not assign papers to students with maximum or minimum word counts anymore. Rather, I use vague language like "about 1,200 words," the approximate length it takes to treat a topic, and I instruct students to use their best judgment in determining a precise length for their argument. Some people have ideas that require them to use more, some are concise writers and can say plenty with fewer words. But more important, teaching introductory philosophy students to write is a matter of teaching them to think long and seriously while simultaneously helping them keep their ideas under control so they do not go off on long tangents. My hope is that vague guidelines force them to develop independent judgment as to the right balance between detail and economy. They often fail miserably. But failures promote learning and growth. I have also become a fan of vague house rules such as "do chores in a timely way" and "keep rooms in reasonable order." Sure, there will be arguments and charges that the chore doer is exploiting a loophole or the enforcer is being arbitrary and nitpicky. People are not completely aligned in their interpretations of *timely* and *reasonable*, but the rules develop a person's knowledge of their own boundaries of timeliness and reasonableness while forcing them to think about other people's boundaries. These kinds of rules require thinking about other people, precisely what living together demands.

> (3) Build mechanisms into the rules and the system that periodically restore discretion as a check on the excesses of legalism, such as earned-discretion clauses.

For instance, enforcers who have worked sufficiently long or have otherwise established reputations for good judgment acquire the ability to make more discretionary decisions on the job. This includes cops who have no excessive-force complaints and prosecutors who hit the right balance of public safety and civil liberty protection and maintain manageable jail populations and lower recidivism levels. Earned discretion gives a way to grant those with wise judgment more power to exercise those judgments when needed. This is not to benefit the wise bureaucrats, but to benefit us, the people they serve.

> (4) Give all enforcers a discretionary budget, an ability to exercise selective, interpretive, or adjudicative discretion up to a certain limit and allow increases in that budget as they show a reputation for good judgment.

One benefit of this system is that legalists can have it their way; the mediocre can continue to trudge along in their by-the-book roles without the power to bring down the entire bureaucracy. However, those who have displayed excellent judgment, the Confucian ideal, will not be hamstrung by mandates, bad rules, or poorly designed systems that do not allow people in the system to make exceptions to rules.

Ideas (3) and (4) respond to the fact that mistrust can be justified. But it prevents that mistrust from being permanently enshrined in the rules themselves. If we build into laws and jobs the ability for trust to be earned back, we can halt our self-destructive march to legalism.

> (5) Bureaucrats ought to have—and citizens are entitled to know—specific moral decision-making frameworks that govern their discretionary decision-making, so we do not hire only by-the-book bureaucrats who have no way of seeing outside the rules of their organization.

Under legalism we expect nothing of our bureaucrats. With restored discretion, we should expect a lot more. Judges who are given a lot of adjudicative discretion must often testify in confirmation hearings about their judicial philosophy. We should ask them specific questions, like how much they weigh victim-impact statements or collateral consequences of conviction or the fact that a defendant is the sole provider for their children. But more importantly, we should institute similar vetting procedures for other positions requiring discretion. We should know of any given beat cop whether they are going to arrest Joey or broker a peace and how they will do it. We should know from the person who is up for a job in the purchasing department whether they will approve a coffee order in various circumstances in which it violates a rule.

Next we should hold bureaucrats accountable to these moral frameworks. Discretion means the opportunity for bad, even catastrophic, decisions. Just because a bad decision is allowed by discretion does not mean people who make those decisions cannot be held accountable for them. Currently cops cannot be held legally liable for failing to enforce a law on a given occasion, but that does not mean they cannot be held morally responsible. To that end, I propose:

(6) In the same way that professions have codes of ethics and professional associations have ethics boards, there should be ethics boards that evaluate discretionary decision-making and inform bureaucrats of how they are falling short. It should be possible to remove individuals for patterns of egregious moral errors, even if discretion legally permits them.

Finally, good discretion needs better science. Referees and umpires in sports go through ongoing training to improve their discretionary call making in basketball and football. They embrace new technologies that help them do it. Doctors have, but could have more, seminars and training in high-stakes decision-making in emergency or ICU contexts or in off-label drug prescribing, all discretionary calls. And judges, prosecutors, and police officers could very well use regular training, like doctors, on the latest in best practices in situations that demand discretion, like whether arresting people of this or that kind has been shown to improve or worsen neighborhood outcomes, like whether methamphetamine is really twice as deadly as some other drug so as to warrant twice the sentence. Discretionary decision-making, when considered a *practice*, rather than a necessary evil, should make use of all the same tools as other practices.

(7) There should be regular training in the latest best practices in areas in which people have discretionary power so that decision-making is informed by the best available empirical evidence.

Han Fei believed that legalism was the antidote to mediocrity. I think legalism is a cause of it. Standardized food, standardized homes, standardized essay grading, and standardized bureaucrats are at best *okay*, merely passable objects to be tolerated. They are never excellent, and they do not inspire excellence.

True, they are better than the worst fears of political philosophers. They are better than famines, tyrants, civil wars, and the complete lack of civil institutions. But that is a very low bar. If you have ever been trapped inside a sprawling bureaucracy, sent to one by-the-book bureaucrat after another to get a permit, medical procedure, or reimbursement approved, you will know how low everyone's expectations are. You will know how helpless everyone inside of that system feels. We're sorry, they will say, but this is the system, these are the rules, we all have to work within them.

No, we do not. We do not have to treat human agency like a venom to civil society, sucking and draining every last bit of it from the institutions that matter the most. We can instead treat agency and the cultivation of its virtuous practice as essential to all people in all jobs, especially the jobs of people in power.

ACKNOWLEDGMENTS

MANY THANKS TO the people who made possible season 4 of *Hi-Phi Nation*, "Crime and Punishment," from which the ideas of this book sprang. This includes Sarah Lustbader; Noa Mendoza-Goot; the Whiting Foundation, who funded the season through their Public Engagement grant; and the many people at Slate audio at the time—Alicia Montgomery, Gabriel Roth, June Thomas, Asha Saluja, Chau Tu, and Dana Stevens.

The people whose stories, ideas, and research form the backbone of this book, and who were also gracious with their time in interviews and phone calls, are Brandon del Pozo, Sarah Seo, Natasha Irving, Luke Hunt, the Honorable Frederic Block, the Honorable Russell Canan, Zachary Hoskins, Lisa Newman-Polk, Thea Johnson, Michelle Madden Dempsey, Aya Gruber, and Lawrence Sherman.

Kelly Rozek served as wise counsel on background throughout the entire research process and has been a lifelong friend and confidante.

Thanks to Alane Mason and Andrew Blitzer at Norton for taking a gamble on a philosophy podcaster like me.

A final thanks to my family, Shanna Andrawis and Darcy Lam, for their patience in hearing out every last story and idea at the dinner table.

NOTES

CHAPTER 1: AT THE CROSSROAD OF PEACE AND FORCE

17 **an essential feature of good policing:** Del Pozo, *The Police and the State*.

23 **alliance on mandatory-arrest:** Gruber, *The Feminist War on Crime*.

23 **As of 2019:** Chin and Cunningham, "Warrantless Domestic Violence Arrest Laws."

24 **mandatory- versus discretionary-arrest policies:** Xie, Lauritsen, and Heimer, "Intimate Partner Violence." See also Hoppe et al., "Mandatory Arrest."

24 **mandatory-arrest policies lead to:** Hirshel, "Domestic Violence Cases."

25 **discretionary- versus mandatory-arrest policies:** Chin and Cunningham, "Warrantless Domestic Violence Arrest Laws."

CHAPTER 3: CHARGING LEFT, CHARGING RIGHT

51 **conviction rate:** "Stacked," *Harvard Law Review*.

53 **particularly abhorrent:** In one famously litigated case, *Alexander v. DeAngelo*, 329 F.3d 912 (7th Cir. 2003), law enforcement had a woman perform oral sex on a target of a sting operation so that they could obtain a semen sample for DNA analysis. This case was famous only because the outcome of litigation was an appellate court decision that such an act was perfectly fine. The number of cases involving young people who end up murdered as "confidential informants" is so numerous that it was used as an argument by a judge on the appellate court to argue that, since even risking someone's murder is within legal bounds, risking someone's health through oral sex is within legal bounds.

54 **extensively reported by ProPublica:** Kohler, "Police Resistance and Politics."

56   **"I have to pursue it"**: "The Good Samaritan," *Radiolab*.

57   **the Good Samaritan laws**: In Ronnie Goldy's case, there might be a high-minded reason for his decision to prosecute the Good Samaritans, but there might not be. Ronnie Goldy was impeached and convicted of state bribery and corruption charges and indicted on federal bribery and corruption charges in the summer of 2023. Sometimes good old-fashioned corruption, like the hope of a bribe, might be a good enough explanation for why a public official acts the way they do.

CHAPTER 4: THE LAWS OF BUREAUDYNAMICS

66   **the guidance value of law**: Endicott, "The Value of Vagueness."

70   **so clause (2) was born**: This story is, of course, fanciful on many different dimensions. Rule making in large bureaucracies is more byzantine than the rules themselves. In the federal government, it involves expert committees, public comment, congressional, presidential, and judicial review, negotiations with lobbyists, and more. See a masterful analysis in Potter, *Bending the Rules*.

72   **the Burger Court in 1983**: The case made Lawson one of the most discussed SCOTUS plaintiffs of the year. He appeared on *Oprah* and other shows to talk about everyday experiences of racism. But the victory was not enough to prevent him from being arrested yet again on a similar vague statute ten years later, this time in Beverly Hills, California. Lawson was pulled over and was ultimately arrested for not providing a driver's license in a timely manner.

73   **"arbitrary domination"**: Machiavelli, *The Prince*.

78   **basic speed law in clause (3)**: How is this possible if it was already voided for vagueness? Because the clause is now employed in the context of a precise maximum speed law, Rudy Stanko's challenge does not apply to the case. For clause (3) to be challenged now, someone has to claim that they were going slower than the maximum speed but was ticketed for going at an unsafe speed and make the case that the conditions made that speed safe. To date, no such successful challenge has been made, in Montana or any state.

79   **a clearly unreasonable expectation**: When I moved from New York back to California, I had to take a written driver's test to allow me to acquire a California driver's license, even though I used to have a California driver's license. I passed the test but missed enough questions to put me in danger

of failing. One question remains particularly memorable. If I want to pass a car and up ahead is an incline or curve, how far away must the incline or curve be for me to pass? The answer, which I missed, is one-third of a mile. This might be a reasonable law, and it might even be reasonable to expect an ordinary person to remember if it were the only one. But in the context of the totality of traffic law, it is completely unreasonable.

CHAPTER 5: MANDATES AND THE NORMALIZATION OF LYING

80 **child-custody and eviction decisions**: Canan, Mize, and Weisberg, *Tough Cases.*

80 **tough case of his own**: "Rough Justice" in Canan, Mize, and Weisberg, *Tough Cases.*

93 **punishment for a conviction**: I cover this case and the philosophical issues it raises in detail on the "Punishment without End" episode of *Hi-Phi Nation.*

95 **are fictions**: Johnson, "Fictional Pleas."

102 **12.5 percent to 25 percent of cases**: Hofer, "Federal Sentencing."

102 **more than doubled**: Yang, "Interjudge Sentencing Disparities." See also Yang, "Free at Last?"

102 **largely due to judicial discretion**: US Sentencing Commission, "Demographic Differences."

102 **at more like two months**: Hofer, "Federal Sentencing," and Yang, "Free at Last?" The differences are due largely to how researchers categorize defendants as being the same for the purpose of comparing their sentences. If two people commit the same crime but one has a long criminal history and the other has none, one study might count that as a same-crime, different-time disparity while another does not.

103 **than they did pre-*Booker***: Lynch, "Booker Circumvention?"

CHAPTER 6: THE COMING OF THE ROBOT RULERS

109 **than ordinary discretionary judgment**: Stevenson, "Assessing Risk Assessment."

110 **sentence structure, and so forth**: Attali and Burstein, "Automated Essay Scoring."

FURTHER READING

Attali, Yigal, and Jill Burstein. "Automated Essay Scoring with E-rater V.2.0." *Journal of Technology, Learning and Assessment* 4, no. 3 (2014).

Canan, Russell, Gregory Mize, and Frederick Weisberg, eds. *Tough Cases: Judges Tell the Stories of Some of the Hardest Decisions They've Ever Made.* New Press, 2018.
This is a riveting book in which judges talk about their often-tortured consciences when presiding over morally fraught cases. It includes Russell Canan's version of the story I present in chapter 5, which I've adapted from an interview I did with Canan.

Chin, Yoo-Mi, and Scott Cunningham. "Revisiting the Effect of Warrantless Domestic Violence Arrest Laws on Intimate Partner Homicides." *Journal of Public Economics* 179, no. 3 (November 2019).
This article gives an updated list of states that have mandatory-, preferred-, and discretionary-arrest policies for domestic violence and their effects on spousal and partner homicides.

Del Pozo, Brandon. *The Police and the State: Security, Social Cooperation, and the Public Good.* Cambridge University Press, 2022.
The arguments in this book owe a great deal to Brandon del Pozo, former New York City police officer; police chief of Burlington, Vermont; philosopher; and current researcher in harm-reduction practices, a combination of expertise few in history can claim. This book represents a unified political philosophy of police discretion that is a model of what every profession ought to have: a theory of good and bad approaches to exercising discretion.

Endicott, Timothy. "The Value of Vagueness." In *Philosophical Foundations of Language and Law*, edited by Andrei Marmor and Scott Soames. Oxford University Press, 2011.
Essentially all of my philosophical vocabulary and discussion of guidance value, process value, the necessity of vague law, and the problem of arbitrariness for precise law comes from this article by philosopher Timothy Endicott.

"The Good Samaritan." *Radiolab*, WNYC Studios. https://radiolab.org/podcast /good-samaritan-2303.

Gruber, Aya. *The Feminist War on Crime: The Unexpected Role of Women's Liberation in Mass Incarceration*. University of California Press, 2021.
This book documents the role of the feminist movement in mandatory-arrest policies in domestic violence as well as other punitive policies in American criminal justice.

Hirshel, J. David. "Domestic Violence Cases: What Research Shows about Arrest and Dual Arrest Rates." NIJ ePub (2008).

Hofer, Paul. "Federal Sentencing after *Booker*." *Crime and Justice* 48 (February 2019).
The most comprehensive data to date about the effects of *Booker* on judicial sentencing comes from this article.

Hoppe, Susan J., Yan Zhang, Brittany E. Hayes, and Matthew A. Bills. "Mandatory Arrest for Domestic Violence and Repeat Offending: A Meta-Analysis." *Aggression and Violent Behavior* 53 (July–August 2020).

Johnson, Thea. "Fictional Pleas," *Indiana Law Journal* 94, no. 3 (2019): 855–900.
This article is where the term "fictional pleas" originates, and it provides a masterful characterization of the era of falsifying factual records in the process of plea bargaining.

Kohler, Jeremy. "Police Resistance and Politics Undercut the Authority of Prosecutors Trying to Reform the Justice System." *ProPublica* (October 11, 2023). https://www.propublica.org/article/police-politicians-undermined -reform-prosecutors-chicago-philadelphia.

The best resource for reporting on progressive prosecutors and the efforts to undermine them is ProPublica. This is one among many articles documenting the ongoing struggle.

Lipsky, Michael. *Street-Level Bureaucracy: Dilemmas of the Individual in Public Service*, 30th ann. ed. Russell Sage Foundation, 2019.
This is the locus classicus of the study of discretion in bureaucracies. While it is not cited in this book, every examination of discretion in bureaucratic decision-making begins with Lipsky.

Lynch, Mona. "Booker Circumvention? Adjudication Strategies in the Advisory Sentencing Guidelines Era." *NYU Review of Law and Social Change*. 43 (2019): 59–107.
This paper is an examination of the effect that the *Booker* decision had on prosecutors and defense attorneys, rather than judicial discretion, and is absolutely central to understanding the true effects of *Booker* since most justice is done outside of the courtroom and view of judges.

Machiavelli, Niccolò. *The Prince*. Penguin Books, 1981.

Potter, Rachel Augustine. *Bending the Rules: Procedural Politicking in the Bureaucracy*. University of Chicago Press, 2019.
Potter is a current academic and former bureaucrat who spent years inside of the US government's sprawling bureaucracies learning and documenting the byzantine procedures behind rule making and rule bending. This book goes through everything you didn't think you needed to know about US government bureaucracy.

"Punishment without End" episode of *Hi-Phi Nation*. https://hiphination. org/season-4-episodes/s4-episode-9-punishment-without-end-june-20th -2020/.

Sherman, Lawrence W., and Richard A. Berk. "The Minneapolis Domestic Violence Experiment." *Police Foundation Reports* (April 1984).
This is the original Minneapolis study by Sherman and Berk that launched the entire mandatory-arrest-policy movement that spread to half of the states in the US.

Sherman, Lawrence W., and Heather M. Harris. "Increased Death Rates of Domestic Violence Victims from Arresting vs. Warning Suspects in the Milwaukee Domestic Violence Experiment (MilDVE)." *Journal of Experimental Criminology* 11, no. 1 (March 2015): 1–20.
This is the retrospective study Sherman conducted documenting the increased rates of early deaths of victims of domestic violence when their partner was arrested.

"Stacked: Where Criminal Charge Stacking Happens—and Where It Doesn't." *Harvard Law Review* 136, no. 5 (March 2023).

Stevenson, Megan. "Assessing Risk Assessment in Action." *Minnesota Law Review* 303, no. 103 (January 2019): 304–84.
The person I've learned the most from about the effects of algorithmic risk assessment in the criminal justice system is Megan Stevenson, who has a series of papers documenting how they work and how they are used in the justice system.

US Sentencing Commission. "Demographic Differences in Sentencing: An Update to the 2012 *Booker* Report." *Federal Sentencing Reporter* 30, no. 3 (2018): 212–29.

Xie, Min, Janet L. Lauritsen, and Karen Heimer. "Intimate Partner Violence in US Metropolitan Areas: The Contextual Influences of Police and Social Services." *Criminology* 50, no. 4 (November 2012): 961–92.

Yang, Crystal S. "Free at Last? Judicial Discretion and Racial Disparities in Federal Sentencing." *Journal of Legal Studies* 44, no. 1 (January 2015): 75–111.

Yang, Crystal S. "Have Interjudge Sentencing Disparities Increased in an Advisory Guidelines Regime? Evidence from *Booker.*" *New York University Law Review* 89, no. 4 (October 2014): 1268–342.
Yang, in addition to Hofer, meticulously documents the effects of *Booker* on various judicial disparities in federal sentencing and shows that how you measure disparities affects the disparities you find.

Zacka, Bernardo. *When the State Meets the Street: Public Service and Moral Agency*. Harvard University Press, 2017.
This award-winning book by an academic and former street-level bureaucrat documents the ways in which moral decision-making pervades the work of street-level bureaucrats.

INDEX

Norton Shorts

BRILLIANCE WITH BREVITY

W. W. Norton & Company has been independent since 1923, when William Warder Norton and Mary (Polly) D. Herter Norton first published lectures delivered at the People's Institute, the adult education division of New York City's Cooper Union. In the 1950s, Polly Norton transferred control of the company to its employees.

One hundred years after its founding, W. W. Norton & Company inaugurates a new century of visionary independent publishing with Norton Shorts. Written by leading-edge scholars, these eye-opening books deliver bold thinking and fresh perspectives in under two hundred pages.

Available Winter 2025

Imagination: A Manifesto by Ruha Benjamin

What's Real About Race?: Untangling Science, Genetics, and Society by Rina Bliss

Offshore: Stealth Wealth and the New Colonialism by Brooke Harrington

Fewer Rules, Better People: The Case for Discretion by Barry Lam

Explorers: A New History by Matthew Lockwood

Wild Girls: How the Outdoors Shaped the Women Who Challenged a Nation by Tiya Miles

The Moral Circle: Who Matters, What Matters, and Why by Jeff Sebo

Against Technoableism: Rethinking Who Needs Improvement by Ashley Shew

Literary Theory for Robots: How Computers Learned to Write by Dennis Yi Tenen

Forthcoming

Mehrsa Baradaran on the racial wealth gap

Merlin Chowkwanyun on the social determinants of health

Daniel Aldana Cohen on eco-apartheid

Jim Downs on cultural healing

Reginald K. Ellis on Black education versus Black freedom

Nicole Eustace on settler colonialism

Agustín Fuentes on human nature

Kelly Lytle Hernandez on racism

Justene Hill Edwards on the history of inequality in America

Destin Jenkins on a short history of debt

Quill Kukla on a new vision of consent

Kelly Lytle Hernández on the immigration regime in America

Natalia Molina on the myth of assimilation

Rhacel Salazar Parreñas on human trafficking

Tony Perry on water in African American culture and history

Beth Piatote on living with history

Ashanté Reese on the transformative possibilities of food

Tracy K. Smith on poetry in an age of technology

Daniel Steinmetz-Jenkins on religion and populism

Onaje X. O. Woodbine on transcendence in sports